D0409630

30-SECOND
POLITICS

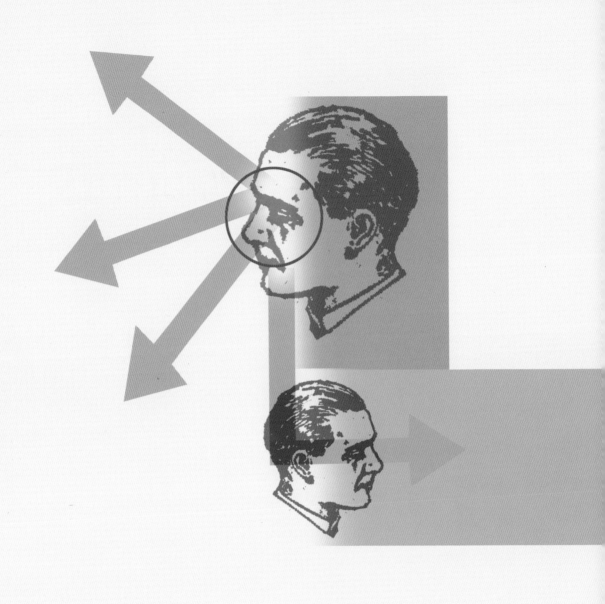

30- SECOND
POLITICS

The 50 most thought-provoking
theories in politics, each
explained in half a minute

Editor
Steven L. Taylor

Contributors
Michael Bailey
Elizabeth Blum
G. Doug Davis
Christopher N. Lawrence
Feng Sun
Steven L. Taylor
Gregory Weeks

Illustrations
Ivan Hissey

ICON

First published in the UK in 2012 by
Icon Books Ltd
Omnibus Business Centre
39–41 North Road, London N7 9DP
email: info@iconbooks.com
www.iconbooks.com

© 2012 by Ivy Press Limited

The editor and contributors
have asserted their moral rights.

No part of this book may be
reproduced in any form, or by
any means, without prior permission
in writing from the publisher.

This book was conceived,
designed and produced by
Ivy Press
Ovest House, 58 West Street
Brighton BN1 2RA, UK
www.ivypress.co.uk

Creative Director **Peter Bridgewater**
Publisher **Jason Hook**
Editorial Director **Caroline Earle**
Art Director **Michael Whitehead**
Designer **Ginny Zeal**
Concept Design **Linda Becker**
Profiles & Glossaries Text **Steve Luck**
Senior Editor **Stephanie Evans**
Project Editor **Jamie Pumfrey**

ISBN: 978-1-84831-403-0

Printed and bound in China

Colour origination by
Ivy Press Reprographics

10 9 8 7 6 5 4

CONTENTS

INTRODUCTION
Steven L. Taylor

Much to the delight of political scientists

everywhere, Aristotle once described the study of politics as the 'master science'. Of course, he did not do so for the purpose of boosting the egos of a bunch of academics, rather he was expressing the notion that studying the interactions of human beings within the confines of political life encompassed the study of practically everything. While perhaps a grandiose formulation on the one hand, on the other consider the following set of issues that fall under the general rubric of politics: war and peace, criminal justice, taxation, safety regulations, civil rights and liberties, trade, abortion, marriage and rules governing scientific enquiry (to name but a few). Given the significance of these types of issues, the rules and structures governing their contents and application directly shape our lives. Put another way: one's daily existence would be very different if one was born in North Korea versus in the South in terms both of material conditions as well as in the realm of rights and privileges. In short: politics matters. This book seeks to be an aid in sorting out the complexity of the political world and the language associated with it.

Aristotle provides a good place to start such a discussion, as he created a simple yet useful typology for classifying **regime types** by looking at the question of who governs: the one, the few or the many. This approach forms the foundation of the opening chapters of this book. The first chapter, Who Governs?, details what government by the one, few or many might look like in **basic terms**. The second, Rule by the Few, goes on to examine specifically

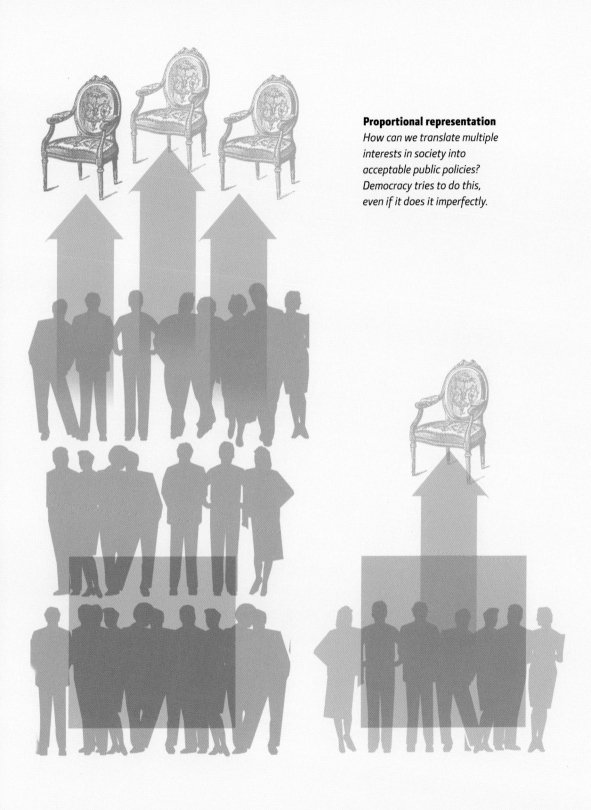

Proportional representation
How can we translate multiple interests in society into acceptable public policies? Democracy tries to do this, even if it does it imperfectly.

regimes wherein the one or the few govern, or what we would call in modern parlance **authoritarian regimes**. From there we move to the question of Rule by the Many – in other words, democratic regimes. This third chapter details the basics of **democratic governance** while the fourth looks specifically at key **elements** of governance, especially of a democratic nature, through the prism of the work of Montesquieu, the French philosopher who heavily influenced the writers of the United States Constitution. Since democracy is the dominant form of government globally at the moment (even if imperfectly executed), more time is devoted to that general topic than any other.

The various **communist theories** are considered next. While it is true that, save for a few exceptions, communism is a dead regime type, the concepts are still relevant to political discourse as the terminology remains with us (not to mention that the current world order was shaped in large part, until only a few decades ago, by these ideas).

Beyond basic regime types and theoretical schools of thought, other elements bear consideration. One is the clear connection between politics and economics, and hence the penultimate chapter, Political Economy, deals with a number of interrelated issues. Another key focus for the study of politics is the question of why states go to war and why they make peace. As such, the final chapter details some key terms and concepts in the realm of **international relations**.

The book provides a lengthy menu of items to sample, yet it offers only a taste of each. Hopefully such samples will inspire further thought, reading and research.

Globalization
A key political challenge in the current era is that we are all becoming increasingly interconnected.

THE BASICS: WHO GOVERNS?

THE BASICS: WHO GOVERNS?
GLOSSARY

absolute power Total authority over every aspect of a state or nation and its inhabitants. The term is usually used with reference to the power of an absolute monarch. Absolute monarchs ruled absolutely in part due to the concept of the divine right of kings, which affirmed that the king's right to rule was derived directly from God.

Arab socialism A political ideology that combines elements of socialism with a pan-Arabic agenda, which seeks to unify the various countries of the Arab world. Although Arab socialism follows many of the social and economic policies of European socialism, it differs by retaining a strong cultural and spiritual Arabic identity.

bourgeoisie A term most often associated with Marxism to describe the owners of the means of production, by which is meant the capitalist upper and middle classes.

city-state An independent state comprising a single city with sovereignty over the surrounding territory. The most famous city-states are those of ancient Greece, such as Sparta, Athens and Thebes. Although most city-states initially existed as monarchies, over time they developed alternative political systems including aristocracies, oligarchies and democracies.

constitutional monarchy A system of government in which the monarch, although head of state, performs only ceremonial and official duties. Most monarchies today exist within the framework of a constitutional parliamentary system in which legislation is enacted through a democratically elected parliament.

enlightened absolutism The absolute power of a monarch who ruled with a consideration to Enlightenment philosophy. Such rulers introduced reforms that encouraged freedom of expression, religious tolerance and the right to own property. Patronage of the arts and the founding of educational establishments were also indicative of enlightened absolutism.

hereditary monarchy A form of monarchy in which the title of king or queen is passed on to the eldest son or daughter, or next nearest blood relative, on the death of the incumbent monarch. Almost all monarchies were and still are based on the hereditary system, although historically male primogeniture, in which boys always inherited before girls, or in which girls were excluded altogether, was common.

Marxism-Leninism A variation of classic Marxist ideology developed by Vladimir Lenin. He identified imperialist trade as providing sufficient wealth via the bourgeoisie to the proletariat, preventing revolution. The proletariat would therefore need to be led to revolution by intellectual and dedicated revolutionaries. Lenin also identified the developing world as the arena for revolutionary action against imperialism. Marxism-Leninism was adopted as the mainstream ideology by the Communist International in 1919.

meritocracy An ideological system of government in which individuals attain positions of responsibility and power by virtue of their ability alone. The idea of a meritocratic system is to prevent nepotism and cronyism, however detractors argue that it's difficult to quantify 'merit'.

mixed economy A term used to describe an economy in which there are both deregulated and regulated elements. Most developed countries, while aiming for a free market in terms of the free movement of goods, labour and so on, include some form of government intervention, whether through subsidies of rail or airlines, or through the provision of welfare.

proletariat A term used in Marxist theory to describe the working class; the proletariat do not own the means of production, and therefore have to sell their labour to survive.

tyrant A ruler with absolute power. Today the term is synonymous with despot, the inference being an authoritarian ruler who governs oppressively and brutally. The term, however, derives from ancient Greece, and simply described someone who seizes power rather than inheriting or constitutionally acceding to it – the tyrant may then have gone on to govern fairly

MONARCHY

the 30-second politics

Hereditary monarchs have existed throughout recorded history and historically claimed that their power to rule comes from God or some other divine source, even in societies that were not organized as theocracies. In practical terms, some monarchs have been so feared (or loved) that they could rule with *absolute* power over their subjects, while others have only been figureheads with real power shared with dukes, earls and princes. During the Napoleonic Wars, the French Emperor Napoleon I even installed 'kings' to govern several of the puppet states he established. Monarchies in the modern world have developed in different directions; those in Europe (except the Vatican City) have become *constitutional* monarchies where the sovereign retains little day-to-day power; the king or queen's actual power is limited by law and tradition, while real power lies in a prime minister chosen by an elected parliament. Others, such as Saudi Arabia and the member states of the United Arab Emirates, still have monarchs who rule their countries directly.

3-SECOND SOUNDBITE
A monarchy is a country, nation or empire that is ruled nominally or absolutely by an hereditary king, queen, sheikh or similar.

3-MINUTE MANIFESTO
While some hereditary monarchies have endured, others have perished – sometimes literally. In some countries, such as the United Kingdom and the Netherlands, the monarch has become an important symbol of national unity; in others, such as Greece and Italy in the 20th century, the monarch was a source of division, leading to their removal. Communism was no friend of monarchies. It resulted in the execution of the Russian royal family, while in other communist countries royals were forced into exile.

RELATED THEORIES
See also
DESPOTISM
page 16
ARISTOCRACY
page 18
THEOCRACY
page 50
IMPERIALISM
page 142

3-SECOND BIOGRAPHIES
CHARLEMAGNE
768–814
King of the Franks

LOUIS XIV
1643–1715
King of France at the height of its absolute monarchy

JUAN CARLOS I
1975–
Presided over the restoration of democracy after Franco

30-SECOND TEXT
Christopher N. Lawrence

'The king reigns, but does not govern.'
JAN ZAMOYSKI

DESPOTISM

the 30-second politics

Despotism (or tyranny) occurs

when a nation or country is ruled by a *tyrant* – a ruler who governs with little regard to popular support or even the best interests of his or her people. Originally the word *turannos* in ancient Greek did not have a negative meaning attached to it – but, as in the case of the later German word *führer*, it only took one bad ruler to make a formerly neutral word *verboten*. At first the word *turannos* only meant that the individual had taken power without accordance to the law; only later did the title include the more modern sense of dictatorial rule as well. Even so the difference between a mere monarch and a tyrant or despot is often highly subjective. The Baron de Montesquieu, writing in *The Spirit of the Laws* in the 18th century, argued that the difference lay in the fact that while the actions of a king would be guided by law and tradition, the rule of a tyrant was arbitrary and capricious; however, more than a few monarchs (such as France's Louis XIV and – in the eyes of the British Parliament at least – England's Charles I) seem to have crossed that line.

3-SECOND SOUNDBITE
A political system in which an often harsh and oppressive ruler wields absolute power.

3-MINUTE MANIFESTO
In the modern world, tyrants are often called dictators or despots instead. They usually claim a legal or moral basis for their rule, most often – but not always – based on a totalitarian or authoritarian ideology, either imported or home-grown, such as Marxism-Leninism, Arab socialism or fascism. However, not every totalitarian or authoritarian state is despotic in nature; some, such as post-Mao China or the Soviet Union after Stalin, have had multiple leaders exercising their overlapping powers collectively as an oligarchy.

RELATED THEORIES
See also

3-SECOND BIOGRAPHIES
PEISISTRATUS
546–527/8 BC
First tyrant of Athens

KIM IL-SUNG
1948–1994
Former president of North Korea, established a cult of personality

SADDAM HUSSEIN
1979–2003
Former president of Iraq

30-SECOND TEXT
Christopher N. Lawrence

'Wherever Law ends, Tyranny begins.'
JOHN LOCKE

ARISTOCRACY

the 30-second politics

3-SECOND SOUNDBITE
Aristocracy means rule by
'the few', whether those
few are the nation's
brightest and best,
wealthy nobles, or a
group of prominent (if
rather frighteningly
inbred) families.

3-MINUTE MANIFESTO
Rhetoric and reality do not
always match up. Labelling
a practice as aristocratic is
almost always a criticism,
yet some features of
modern democracies such
as elections of rulers (where
campaigns promote the
candidates' superior
qualities) and lifetime
appointments of judges
actually smuggle elements
of aristocracy into the
practice of democracy. The
more democratic selection
of rulers by lot – how jurors
are selected in the United
States and United Kingdom
for example – is rarely
employed at national level.

Everyone has had a memorable
moment while watching the evening television
news when one wonders, 'How did *that* clown
get elected? *I* could do a better job than him!'
That judgment, whether we recognized it at the
time or not, is essentially aristocratic in nature.
Aristocracy is rule by the few, and its
justification is that not everyone is equally
equipped to rule and most people are altogether
unfit for ruling. Governing is an exceedingly
tricky business that shapes the quality of life of
every citizen, and to do it well takes brains,
considerable preparation, training or, ideally, all
of the above. Aristocracy is therefore grounded
in the idea of meritocracy – the idea that only
the wisest and most virtuous persons should be
allowed access to the reins of power. Virtually
everyone acknowledges that some rulers are
better than others, and some people are more
fit than others to rule, so the popular resistance
to embracing aristocracy more openly stems not
so much from its idea as its practice. Almost
from its inception in ancient Greece, aristocracy
became intertwined with rule by leading wealthy
families whose power and wealth were
buttressed by laws that almost always led to
opulence but only occasionally
led to justice for the citizenry.

RELATED THEORIES
See also
MONARCHY
page 14
OLIGARCHY
page 22
PATRIMONIALISM
page 46

3-SECOND BIOGRAPHIES
PLATO
428–348 BC
Greek philosopher who
advocated rule by the wise

ALEXIS DE TOCQUEVILLE
1805–1859
French aristocrat who made
keen observations on democracy

30-SECOND TEXT
Michael E. Bailey

*[In aristocratic nations],
'the family represents
the land, and the land
the family, perpetuating
its name, origin, glory,
power and virtue. It is
an imperishable witness
to the past, a precious
earnest of the future.'*
ALEXIS DE TOCQUEVILLE

384 BC
Born in Stageira

367 BC
Attended Plato's Academy
in Athens

343 BC
Engaged as tutor to the
future Alexander the Great

335 BC
Established the Lyceum
in Athens

322 BC
Fled Athens due to
anti-Macedonian
sentiment and died
later that year in Euboea.

ARISTOTLE

'Now it is evident that the form of government is best in which every man, whoever he is, can act best and live happily'.

It could have been Jefferson or perhaps John Locke from the Enlightenment, but this quote is taken from Aristotle's treatise *Politics* and illustrates the profound impact this ancient Greek philosopher has made on modern Western philosophy and political theory.

Born in 384 BC, Aristotle was from a family of aristocratics. At the age of 18 he attended Plato's Academy in Athens and spent the next 20 years there. Around the time of Plato's death in 348 BC, Aristotle left Athens and travelled through Anatolia. In 343 BC Philip II of Macedon engaged Aristotle to tutor his son, the future Alexander the Great.

Aristotle returned to Athens in 335 BC and set up his own school, the Lyceum. It is the ensuing dozen years that saw him compose his most influential works, among them treatises on ethics, nature, philosophy, poetry and politics.

Aristotle's *Politics* is roughly organized into eight books. It covers a vast range of political concepts, but perhaps its greatest significance today lies in its examination of the responsibility of power. In Book IV Aristotle weighs up the pros and cons of three 'constitutions', those ruled by 'one', 'few' or 'many'. A monarchy (one), he argues, can be successful if the king is moral, but can easily degrade into tyranny if he is not. A state ruled by the aristocracy (few) becomes an oligarchy when it caters only for the interests of the rich, while allowing everyone to rule (many) will result in the exclusion of the needs of all others except the poor. His conclusion? The fairest constitution is a mixed 'polity' of rich and poor.

OLIGARCHY

the 30-second politics

An oligarchy is a ruling elite

governing for its own self-interest rather than for the interest of society as whole. Aristotle developed the concept as one of his categories of different city-states. In an oligarchic political system, the economic and military power rests within a small group of individuals, either literally families or just tightknit groups with long-standing mutual interests. They control the lion's share of the wealth, so the gap between rich and poor is large, and the majority of the population has little political voice. By definition it is anti-democratic, and even when elections occur, they are not allowed to challenge the status quo. If the oligarchy is threatened, then it represses or overthrows whatever political forces are responsible. The political system is therefore set up in a way that perpetuates the status quo. Prominent modern examples include much of Central America and the Caribbean. In countries such as Guatemala, Haiti or Honduras, long histories of elite rule – even extending back into the colonial period – have left oligarchies firmly in control. Large landowning families go back generations, and the structure of power has changed very little over time.

3-SECOND SOUNDBITE
An oligarchy is a political system in which a small ruling elite takes resources from everyone and gives back only to its own.

3-MINUTE MANIFESTO
Aristotle argued that an aristocracy was also rule by the few, but was not oligarchic because it ruled with the common good as a goal. It is also very easy for an oligarchy to be patrimonial, as the few do not distinguish between their interests and those of the State.

RELATED THEORIES
See also
ARISTOCRACY
page 18
AUTHORITARIANISM
page 28
PATRIMONIALISM
page 46

3-SECOND BIOGRAPHIES
PLATO
428–348 BC
Greek philosopher who defined oligarchy as rule by the wealthy

ARISTOTLE
384–322 BC
see pages 20–21

GAETANO MOSCA
1858–1941
Italian theorist who wrote about elite rule

30-SECOND TEXT
Gregory Weeks

'The tyranny of a prince in an oligarchy is not so dangerous to the public welfare as the apathy of a citizen in a democracy.'
MONTESQUIEU

DEMOCRACY

the 30-second politics

Democracy is simultaneously
a simple yet highly contested concept. Of
course, we all like the idea of people governing
themselves, but the question becomes: how?
Should all the people govern directly or should
they elect representatives to govern on their
behalf? And if representatives are to be
selected, by what method will that take place?
For that matter, who are 'the people'? The word
democracy derives from the two Greek words:
demos ('the people') and *kratos* ('to rule'). It is
both a very ancient and very modern concept.
Plato and Aristotle discussed democracy
and both saw it as a problematic type of
government in which the poor would use their
numeric advantage to tear down the wealthy.
Democracy as a viable form of government only
came into existence in the late 1700s – early
1800s and did not come into full maturity until
the 20th century, when universal voting rights
for all citizens regardless of race, gender or
income became the norm. Modern democracy
exists by having power derive from the people
who, in turn, delegate that power to elected
representatives. Democracy has become the
dominant form of government in the world,
although the exact quality of any given
democracy is often a topic for debate.

3-SECOND SOUNDBITE
Democracy is government
of, by and for the people.

3-MINUTE MANIFESTO
Some say countries such
as the United States or
France are republics, not
democracies. It is indeed
true that these countries
do not have direct
democracy where
everyone participates in
government, nor does the
majority always get its
way. A republic is basically
government without a
king with power from the
people. James Madison
used the term 'republic'
in *The Federalist Papers*
to mean a system with
elected representatives.
The terms are largely
synonymous in modern
language. However,
some countries that call
themselves 'republics' do
not allow the population
a say in governance.

RELATED THEORIES
See also
REPRESENTATIVE DEMOCRACY
page 58
CLASSICAL LIBERALISM
page 64
SOCIAL DEMOCRACY
page 74
PARLIAMENTARY DEMOCRACY
page 92

3-SECOND BIOGRAPHIES
JOHN STUART MILL
1806–1873
A major contributor on issues of
liberty and representation

ROBERT DAHL
1915–
A significant 20th-century
analyst of democracy

LARRY DIAMOND
1954–
A key scholar on democracy
worldwide

30-SECOND TEXT
Steven L. Taylor

*'Democracy is the only
system that persists in
asking the powers that
be whether they are the
powers that ought to be.'*
WINSTON CHURCHILL

POPULAR SOVEREIGNTY

the 30-second politics

3-SECOND SOUNDBITE
With popular sovereignty power comes from the governed, not from the governors.

3-MINUTE MANIFESTO
Most modern governments claim their legitimacy comes from popular support, even if there are no procedures in place to ensure that the people have any meaningful control over their rulers. For example, many of the Latin American military dictatorships of the 20th century and the similar, current military dictatorship in Burma (Myanmar), have claimed that their rule is in the best interests of the citizenry and on their behalf.

Popular sovereignty is based on the idea that all legitimate political power comes from the people who are governed, instead of a divine or external source. The concept of popular sovereignty is connected to the idea of a 'social contract' between the people and their government, as expressed in the writings of Enlightenment philosophers Thomas Hobbes, John Locke and Jean-Jacques Rousseau – that the people agree to be governed, in exchange for their rulers' protection of their personal safety, freedom and property. If the rulers were to abuse their power, then people would have the right to rebel. Theoretically any form of government where the ruler or ruling elite governs in the interest and with the consent of the people would reflect popular sovereignty; even an absolute dictatorship could theoretically govern benevolently – this idea has at times been called 'enlightened absolutism' or 'benevolent dictatorship'. However, the idea of popular sovereignty today is most strongly associated with representative democracy and constitutional government, which generally guarantee popular consent for those who rule through the ballot box.

RELATED THEORIES
See also
DEMOCRACY
page 24
ANARCHISM
page 56
MAJORITARIANISM
page 60
SOCIAL DEMOCRACY
page 74

3-SECOND BIOGRAPHIES
JOHN I OF ENGLAND
1199–1216
Signed the Magna Carta (Great Charter), which recognized limits on royal power

THOMAS JEFFERSON
1743–1826
Author of the *Declaration of Independence*

30-SECOND TEXT
Christopher N. Lawrence

'Governments must be conformable to the nature of the governed; governments are even a result of that nature.'
GIOVANNI BATTISTA VICO

AUTHORITARIANISM

the 30-second politics

Authoritarianism is a broad category that encompasses any government where the ultimate power to make decisions for a society is vested in a specific person or a privileged class or group. The decision-makers in question have their power because they belong to a particular family (such as in aristocracies or monarchies), the clerical class (such as in a theocracy), or to some other specific power sphere (such as the military or the landowning class). Some authoritarian governments exercise brutal control over the population while others may take on the appearance of democracy by allowing political groups to form but not to have any real power, and may even hold sham elections (the results of which always favour the governing power). In basic terms the issue of whether a regime is authoritarian or not is whether those who govern have to take into consideration the will and interests of the citizens as defined by those citizens themselves. In other words: can the public at large hold governing elites responsible for the decisions that they make or can those elites ultimately ignore the will of the public? When those who govern are not accountable to the people they govern, a regime is authoritarian.

3-SECOND SOUNDBITE
Authoritarianism is rule by the one or the few.

3-MINUTE MANIFESTO
While authoritarianism is frequently associated with the more extreme examples (such as Hitler's Germany) it is important to remember that there is a wide spectrum of authoritarian government types and not all of them are extreme. Nor should one assume that just because a country holds elections that the country in question is democratic. For example, elections have been held in places such as the Soviet Union, Castro's Cuba and Saddam Hussein's Iraq.

RELATED THEORIES
See also
ONE-PARTY RULE
page 36
FASCISM
page 38
TOTALITARIANISM
page 44
THEOCRACY
page 50

3-SECOND BIOGRAPHIES
HANNAH ARENDT
1906–1975
Political philosopher who specialized in the study of totalitarianism

JUAN J. LINZ
1926–
Political theorist and the author of *Totalitarian and Authoritarian Regimes*

30-SECOND TEXT
Steven L. Taylor

'As virtue is necessary in a republic, and in a monarchy honour, so fear is necessary in a despotic government.'
MONTESQUIEU

CLASS CONFLICT

the 30-second politics

Class conflict (or class struggle)
is the theory, usually associated with Marxist or
communist thought, that a capitalist, industrial
society inevitably would lead to a conflict
between the proletariat, the working class
whose labour led to the production of goods,
and who were paid a wage for their labour, and
the bourgeoisie, the middle and upper classes
who owned the capital or means of production
and who profited from their use to produce
goods. Karl Marx and Friedrich Engels, in
The Communist Manifesto and other writings,
argued that the proletariat did not receive their
fair share of the benefits from their labour – in
other words, the bourgeoisie were paying
labourers only a fraction of the true value of
their labour and pocketing the difference.
Marx and Engels believed that this economic
relationship amounted to a form of exploitation,
and that the proletariat should instead own the
means of production themselves – thereby
reaping the benefits and cutting out the
middleman. To do so in practice would require
a revolutionary change in the State and society,
in order both to dispossess the bourgeoisie of
their property and ensure the State would not
intervene to protect that property from seizure
by the proletariat.

RELATED THEORIES
See also
COMMUNISM
page 102

MARXISM
page 104

LENINISM
page 108

3-SECOND BIOGRAPHIES
KARL MARX
1818–1883
Co-author of *The Communist Manifesto*

FRIEDRICH ENGELS
1820–1895
See pages 106–7

THOMAS MÜNTZER
1488–1525
Reformation theologian, a
leader of the Peasants' War

30-SECOND TEXT
Christopher N. Lawrence

3-SECOND SOUNDBITE
Class conflict results when
those who do all the work
rise up against those who
have all the money.

3-MINUTE MANIFESTO
Class conflict exists in a
number of guises – from
the largely failed attempts
to implement Marxism (in
various forms) in Central
and Eastern Europe, Cuba
and East Asia, to more
moderate efforts to create
mixed economies. Even in
countries most associated
with capitalism, such as
the United States, the
right of labourers to
organize collectively to
promote their common
interest – and thus to
institutionalize 'class
conflict' – is protected by
law, although the relative
strength of labour unions
in capitalist societies has
been in decline since the
Second World War.

*'Let the revolting
distinction of rich and
poor disappear once
and for all ... '*
FRANÇOIS NOËL BABEUF

RULE BY THE FEW

RULE BY THE FEW
GLOSSARY

annexation The incorporation of one, usually smaller, state or territory into an existing state or territory, often undertaken with the use or threat of force. The annexing state then seeks to legitimize its sovereignty through international bodies.

Anschluss The annexation of Austria by Nazi Germany in 1938. Despite this action contravening the Treaty of Versailles, Britain and France accepted the unification with only mild objection.

Aryan Originally an ethno-linguistic term to define those people who speak one of the Indo-European languages, the term was hijacked by the Nazi Party to refer to a 'master race' of people specifically with northern European ancestry. It was a means of differentiating 'Aryans' from 'Semitic' peoples.

autocracy A form of government in which one person has uncontrolled and unlimited authority. Today the term is synonymous with despotism, tyranny or dictatorship.

Axis powers The coalition headed by Germany, Italy (in Europe) and Japan (in the Pacific) during the Second World War, in opposition to the Allied forces headed by the United States, the Soviet Union and Great Britain.

clientelism A social and/or political practice in which politically aspirational rich and powerful individuals ('patrons') ensure that public resources, in the form of, for example, road or rail infrastructure or building contracts, are directed toward a section of the population ('clients') in return for their support, which may take the form of votes or attendance at political rallies.

divine right of kings A political and religious belief which affirmed that monarchs derive their right to rule directly from God, and that they are answerable only to God. Reinforcing royal absolutism, the doctrine was most influential in England and France during the 16th and 17th centuries, but waned following the Glorious Revolution (1688) in England and the French and American revolutions of the late 18th century.

fasces A symbol of legal authority dating back to the Roman Republic. It comprised a bundle of long sticks tied together to form a cylinder, usually with a long-handled axe included among the sticks with the blade projecting from the top or from one side. Mussolini utilized both the symbol and the word fasces when he formed a fascist movement in Italy in 1914.

hegemony The political and/or cultural dominance of one group, state or nation over others, usually through economic, technological or military superiority, but also often accompanied by cooperative trade. The Italian Marxist theorist Antonio Gramsci used the term to describe the dominance of one class over another, to the point at which the subordinate class accepts the world order of the dominant class as 'natural'.

Mandate of Heaven A Chinese political and social philosophy dating back to the advent of the Zhou Dynasty (c. 1050 BC). Similar to the European 'divine right of kings', the Mandate of Heaven asserted that rulers were granted the right to rule with divine approval. However, the right to rule was only divinely granted if the ruler governed well – if a dynasty fell, it was supposed that the right to rule had been withdrawn due to poor governance.

neo-Nazism A term used to describe any extreme right-wing movement that shares some of the political values of those of Nazi Germany. Although most neo-Nazi groups are restricted to Europe, with anti-Semitism, xenophobia and strident nationalism as recurring themes, white supremacist groups also exist in other parts of the world.

politicize The act of turning a non-political issue into a political one. Important scientific concerns, such as global warming, or social moral issues such as abortion or the legalization of certain drugs, are so pervasive and polarizing that politicians either feel obliged or are specifically requested to put forward an opinion. The term also applies to individuals or groups who are motivated or encouraged to think in a political way.

propaganda Communication that is used to further the cause of a political view or group. The information, which can be relayed via newspapers, leaflets, television or radio broadcasts, or even via the internet, is usually biased or even fabricated.

sultanism A form of autocracy, wherein the ruler governs with absolute authority. The term is derived from the word 'sultan', a Muslim sovereign.

Third Reich The name given to Germany by Hitler and the Nazis when they seized power until the end of the Second World War. Reich is German for 'empire', and Hitler's Third Reich followed the First Reich of the Holy Roman Empire (962–1806) and the Second Reich, Bismarck's unified Imperial Germany (1871–1918).

ONE-PARTY RULE

the 30-second politics

One-party rule is a political system in which only one party is allowed to participate, or where restrictive electoral rules make it essentially impossible for any other party to enter the system. The party controls the levers of government and uses state resources to ensure compliance through force but also though propaganda and by providing benefits through patron-client networks. Such systems are clearly non-democratic, but can be quite durable because, unlike a personalistic dictatorship, there is a bureaucratic structure in place that better mediates between the rulers and the ruled. Communist dictatorships constitute the most prominent contemporary examples, where the Communist Party is an elite organization that allows for no political competition. It is important to note, however, that such systems can occur anywhere on the ideological spectrum. There can also be different relationships between dictators and the party, where in some cases the party exerts huge influence (the Soviet Union) while in others the leader wields the power (Cuba). Even in the latter, however, the party plays a central role acting as a go-between for the demands of the ruled and the dictates of the ruler.

3-SECOND SOUNDBITE
A system of government in which only a single political party is invited to the party.

3-MINUTE MANIFESTO
One-party systems should not be confused with dominant-party systems, in which one party is hegemonic but allows other parties to exist and—to a controlled degree—to compete. Mexico from 1929 to 2000 is an example, as is present-day Zimbabwe. They are less rigid but are also non-democratic.

RELATED THEORIES
See also
AUTHORITARIANISM
page 28
COMMUNISM
page 102

3-SECOND BIOGRAPHIES
ROBERT MUGABE
1924–
President of Zimbabwe

KIM JONG IL
1941–2011
Former leader of North Korea

30-SECOND THEORY
Geoffrey Weeks

"The possession of power over others is inherently destructive both to the possessor of the power and to those over whom it is exercised."

GEORGE D. HERRON

FASCISM

the 30-second politics

Fascism is a radical and totalitarian nationalistic governing philosophy that has its origins in Italy under Benito Mussolini and also emerged in different forms in Adolf Hitler's Germany and Francisco Franco's Spain. It is an illiberal regime type, insofar as it denies the significance and rights of the individual and expects citizens to function together in a corporate fashion for the glory of the State. Fascism is defined as much by what it opposes as what it supports: it is anti-modern, anti-rationality, anti-democratic and vehemently anti-communist. Fascism is also militaristic and espouses an imperialistic, expansionistic foreign policy. The use of military symbolism as a means of underscoring the importance and power of the State is a common staple of fascist governments. The source of the name fascism, as coined by Benito Mussolini, was the fasces – a Roman symbol consisting of a bundle of wooden sticks combined with an axe blade. Mussolini adopted the symbol because it both recalled the glory and power of ancient Rome and because of the similarity between the word fasces and the Italian word for bundle or group (*fascio*) – emphasizing the notion of power and strength in unity.

3-SECOND SOUNDBITE
Under fascism the State is all and therefore the individual is nothing.

3-MINUTE MANIFESTO
Fascism lacks the strong philosophical and theoretical underpinning of other ideologies that it opposes. With the defeat of the Axis powers in the Second World War, fascism as a viable model for government essentially disappeared from the world. These days the term is usually deployed as a political insult or as a warning about a particular policy or group (sometimes accurately, but often the term is used in a very vague, ill-defined fashion).

RELATED THEORIES
See also
AUTHORITARIANISM
page 28
NAZISM
page 42
TOTALITARIANISM
page 44

3-SECOND BIOGRAPHIES
GIOVANNI GENTILE
1875–1944
Political theorist

BENITO MUSSOLINI
1883–1945
see pages 40–41

ADOLF HITLER
1889–1945
German dictator

GENERALISSIMO
FRANCISCO FRANCO
1892–1975
Spanish dictator

30-SECOND TEXT
Steven L. Taylor

'Fascism should rightly be called corporatism, as it is the merger of corporate and government power.'
BENITO MUSSOLINI

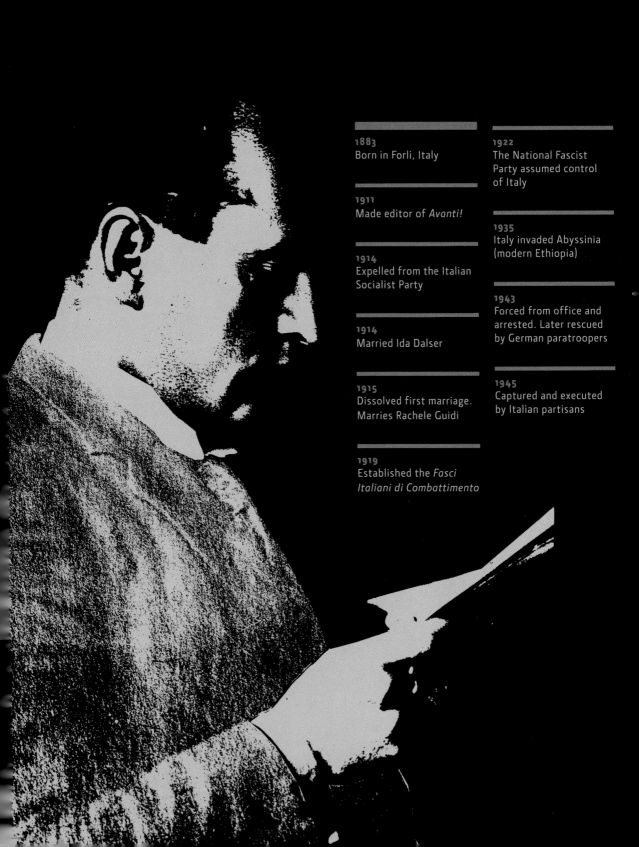

1883
Born in Forli, Italy

1911
Made editor of *Avanti!*

1914
Expelled from the Italian
Socialist Party

1914
Married Ida Dalser

1915
Dissolved first marriage.
Marries Rachele Guidi

1919
Established the *Fasci
Italiani di Combattimento*

1922
The National Fascist
Party assumed control
of Italy

1935
Italy invaded Abyssinia
(modern Ethiopia)

1943
Forced from office and
arrested. Later rescued
by German paratroopers

1945
Captured and executed
by Italian partisans

BENITO MUSSOLINI

For many, the overriding image of fascism is the swastika of Nazi Germany; but in fact fascism emerged out of Italy, and the man responsible was Benito Mussolini.

Mussolini was born in 1883. His father was a blacksmith, socialist and proud nationalist. By his early twenties Mussolini was active in the Italian socialist movement, editing and writing for socialist periodicals, and in 1911 he became editor of the Socialist Party newspaper *Avanti!*, a role in which he excelled.

The outbreak of the First World War was decisive for Mussolini. Although initially opposed to war, he later became a vociferous supporter. He saw it as an opportunity for Italy to assert itself in Europe. The Italian Socialist Party, however, was anti-intervention, and Mussolini was expelled from the Party in 1914. During the War Mussolini denounced socialism as having failed Italy, and in 1919 he formed the *Fasci Italiani di Combattimento* (Italian Combat Squad).

Mussolini's fascism, with its powerful nationalist message and corporate 'third-way' economic policies, gained wide support across all classes. In 1922, with the tacit support of the king, Mussolini's National Fascist Party seized control. Once in power Mussolini used propaganda and violent coercion to advance the cause of the Fascist Party, banning all opposition parties and in essence establishing a dictatorship. Despite his posturing brutality, Mussolini was popular and his programme of public works widely supported.

Mussolini's relationship with Hitler was never comfortable. The Nazi brand of fascism, with its anti-Semitic and eugenic overtones, did not appeal to Mussolini, even though he introduced anti-Semitic legislation. The alliance with Germany in the Second World War was pragmatic and opportunistic – he believed Hitler would win the war and advance the cause of the Italian Empire. After initial success, by 1942 Axis forces were in retreat, and in 1943 Mussolini, now deeply unpopular at home, was forced from office and arrested. Despite being rescued and used as a figurehead in a new fascist regime, he was captured by Italian partisans in 1945 and executed.

NAZISM

the 30-second politics

A variant of fascism, Nazism
was a totalitarian ideology that mixed extreme
nationalism with racism and military expansionism.
The word 'Nazi' derives from an abbreviation
of the National Socialist German Workers' Party
(*Nationalsozialistische Deutsche Arbeiterpartei*),
which was the party of Adolf Hitler when he
was appointed to the Chancellorship in 1933.
Once in power, the Nazis governed Germany as
a one-party totalitarian state. The Nazi ideology
was illiberal, anti-Semitic, anti-Marxist and
stridently nationalist. A key element of Hitler's
Nazism was the notion that the Germanic people
should be united into a single empire (*Reich*).
The first major move in this direction was the
annexation of Austria (known as the *Anschluss*)
followed by the acquisition of portions of
Czechoslovakia as a result of the Munich
Agreement (based on the logic that the large
population of ethnically German residents should
be united with Germany), and the military
conquest of Poland. Nazism unmoored from
German nationalism is largely an ideology of
white supremacy with militant elements but
lacking a coherent philosophy (and is often
referred to as neo-Nazism). As a viable regime
type it died along with Hitler's Third Reich.
Nazism in Germany was heavily linked to the cult
of the personality that emerged around Hitler.

3-SECOND SOUNDBITE
Nazism equals fascism plus
violent anti-Semitism and
militant pan-Germanic
nationalism.

3-MINUTE MANIFESTO
In his book, *Mein Kampf*
(*My Struggle*), Hitler
segmented the human race
into three groups: the
creators of culture (the
Aryans), the destroyers of
culture (the Jews, gypsies,
homosexuals and a variety
of other groups), and the
conveyors of culture
(everyone else). His theory
of race led him to believe
that the Aryans must rule
and that the Jews (and
others he deemed
subhuman) must be
exterminated.

RELATED THEORIES
See also
AUTHORITARIANISM
page 28
FASCISM
page 38
TOTALITARIANISM
page 44

3-SECOND BIOGRAPHIES
FREDERICK NIETZSCHE
1844–1900
German philosopher whose
work is thought by some to have
inspired Nazism

BENITO MUSSOLINI
1883–1945
See pages 40–1

MARTIN HEIDEGGER
1889–1976
German philosopher closely
associated with the Nazi Party

30-SECOND TEXT
Steven L. Taylor

*'Power is the
supreme law.'*
ADOLF HITLER

TOTALITARIANISM

the 30-second politics

A totalitarian system is a type of dictatorship in which the ruling elite exert power not only over the political aspects of their citizens' lives, but over private life as well. The term was first used to describe fascism in the 1920s, but is now more commonly associated with communist systems. The State directs the actions of everyone to ensure that – in theory at least – every member of society is working as part of an organic whole organized by the central authority, with no opposition or political competition allowed. The State imposes strict control over every organization, association and group, and even determines where people are allowed to live or travel. Such a system is also characterized by symbolic demonstrations of unity, with orchestrated parades, ceremonies and other public displays of support. As a result, all of society is politicized, and the line between the State and society is blurred. As the political theorist Hannah Arendt has argued, the State destroys all competing interests and seeks to dominate individuals from within. The highest profile contemporary example is North Korea, where extreme levels of security, combined with effective propaganda and no access to the outside world, provides the State with near total control over the population.

3-SECOND SOUNDBITE
A type of government that tries to control everything, from high politics all the way down to its subjects' very thoughts.

3-MINUTE MANIFESTO
Given globalization and the broad access to technology, totalitarianism is increasingly difficult to maintain, and sometimes its grip gradually loosens. That can mean such dictatorships become authoritarian, in which political life is controlled, but private life is not as long as it does not become political. The term 'post-totalitarian' denotes countries that underwent a transition away from totalitarianism.

RELATED THEORIES
See also
DESPOTISM
page 16
AUTHORITARIANISM
page 28
FASCISM
page 38

3-SECOND BIOGRAPHIES
HANNAH ARENDT
1906–1975
Political theorist who specialized in the study of totalitarianism

KIM IL SUNG
1912–1994
Creator of the totalitarian North Korean political system

JUAN LINZ
1926–
Political scientist known for his work on authoritarianism

30-SECOND TEXT
Gregory Weeks

'Totalitarianism has discovered a means of dominating and terrorizing human beings from within.'
HANNAH ARENDT

PATRIMONIALISM

the 30-second politics

Patrimonialism is a style of ruling a country in which there is little or no distinction between the private interests of the ruler and the public interest – in other words, the 'private' and the 'official' are one and the same. When rulers control all the State's resources, they are able to utilize them according to their own whims. By definition, this arrangement is both undemocratic and autocratic. It is an extreme version of 'clientelism', which refers to a patron-client relationship between ruler and the ruled, with resources flowing downward and political support upward. The term patrimonialism was coined by Max Weber, who analyzed the arbitrary decisions made by members of the royalty who had little or no constraints on their behaviour. His focus was on early modern Europe – from the late 15th century to the late 18th century. Family members, rather than bureaucracies, make all binding decisions. All government officials depend entirely upon their personal relationship with the rulers. Such rulers use whatever force necessary to enforce compliance. That in turn also leads to instability because the only way to enact change is to overthrow the rulers.

RELATED THEORIES
See also
OLIGARCHY
page 22
AUTHORITARIANISM
page 28

3-SECOND SOUNDBITE
Sometimes those who rule continue expanding their power until their interests and those of the State are one and the same.

3-MINUTE MANIFESTO
Max Weber referred to extreme versions of patrimonialism as 'sultanism'. A prominent updated version of the concept includes neo-patrimonialism, which refers to contemporary political systems that are not monarchies but still exhibit the features of traditional patrimonialism. Examples of neo-patrimonial systems exist in regions of Africa, South America and the Middle East.

3-SECOND BIOGRAPHIES
MAX WEBER
1864–1920
German sociologist and influential political economist

ANASTASIO SOMOZA GARCIA
1896–1956
Established a sultanistic dynasty in Nicaragua

FRANÇOIS 'PAPA DOC' DUVALIER
1907–1971
Sultanistic dictator of Haiti

30-SECOND TEXT
Gregory Weeks

'Indeed, you won the elections, but I won the count.'
ANASTASIO SOMOZA GARCIA

PRAETORIANISM

the 30-second politics

Praetorianism often refers to

military rule, but can also reflect a very strong military influence over politics. The term dates back to the Praetorian Guard of the Roman Empire, a collection of soldiers in charge of protecting the political leadership. Over time the Guard became increasingly autonomous and powerful, assassinating emperors and elevating others to power. In the contemporary context, it reflects a situation in which the armed forces are politicized, often becoming political arbiters, and at times assuming full control over the political system to rule directly. As such, military leaders consider themselves more able than civilians in both military and political matters. The phenomenon is clearly associated with weak elite commitment to democracy, fragile political institutions, ideological polarization, political elite ties to the military leadership and a general sense of the military's legitimacy in ruling. Gradually, the military's dominant role becomes entrenched, and it remains a central political actor, particularly in times of political or economic crisis. In present-day Pakistan, for example, the army hovers over the political system, and its political leaders must ensure they maintain military support or face overthrow. An even more striking example is Bolivia, where there have been a staggering 193 coups since independence in 1825.

RELATED THEORIES
See also
DESPOTISM
page 16
AUTHORITARIANISM
page 28

3-SECOND SOUNDBITE
The military believes it often knows better than civilians how to run a country.

3-MINUTE MANIFESTO
Praetorianism is most evident in the developing world and is cited most often in regions such as Latin America, South Asia and sub-Saharan Africa. In many countries, the military was the strongest political institution at the time of independence, and therefore continued to mediate civilian political conflict well into the post-independence period.

3-SECOND BIOGRAPHIES
AUGUSTO PINOCHET
1915–2006
Former military dictator of Chile

SAMUEL P. HUNTINGTON
1927–2008
Author of *The Soldier and the State*

PERVEZ MUSHARRAF
1943–
Former army commander and president of Pakistan

30-SECOND TEXT
Gregory Weeks

'Sometimes democracy must be bathed in blood.'
AUGUSTO PINOCHET

THEOCRACY

the 30-second politics

Theocracy is rule by God, either directly, or via earthly representation in the form of priests. It is not the same as a state religion, which works alongside political rule. It implies that the power to govern is derived from God, and that whoever is governing is a conduit for God's laws and instructions. In some examples, the same hierarchy administers both the religious and the political affairs of a country. In others, there are two systems, but the secular is subservient to the religious. Most examples of theocracy are historical. The Israelites of biblical times lived under a theocracy in which they were governed by Mosaic law, which was handed directly from God to Moses; and early Islam was ruled by Muhammad as the recipient of the law given by Allah. Renaissance popes combined their role as the vicar of God with great secular power. In medieval Europe, and until the time of Cromwell in England, the 'divine right of kings' held sway; it was thought that kings derived their right to rule from God alone, and were therefore answerable only to God. Ancient Chinese emperors ruled under the Mandate of Heaven, which could be withdrawn if an emperor proved too despotic and transferred to a more deserving candidate.

3-SECOND SOUNDBITE
If God is for us, who can be against us?

3-MINUTE MANIFESTO
The term 'theocracy' was invented by Josephus (38–100 BC) specifically to describe the ancient Hebrew constitution based on the concept that God's laws were handed to Moses carved on tablets of stone. While its literal meaning, 'rule of God', seems easy to grasp, the blend of the secular and the sacred in terms of actual practice would need a book the size of the Bible to discuss its implications.

RELATED THEORIES
See also
MONARCHY
page 14
OLIGARCHY
page 22
AUTHORITARIANISM
page 28

3-SECOND BIOGRAPHIES
POPE BENEDICT XVI
1927–
Head of State, Vatican City

ALI HOSEINI-KHAMENEI
1939–
Supreme Leader of Islamic Republic of Iran

MULLAH MUHAMMAD OMAR
1959–
Leader of the Taliban, ruler in Afghanistan 1996–2001

30-SECOND TEXT
Steven L. Taylor

' "Theocracy" has always been the synonym for a bleak and narrow, if not a fierce and blood-stained tyranny. '
WILLIAM ARCHER

RULE BY THE MANY

RULE BY THE MANY
GLOSSARY

coalition In a parliamentary democracy, a government that is made up of two or more political parties. If one party is unable to form a majority in the parliament, passing legislation becomes a hit-and-miss affair, therefore usually the party with the greatest number of elected representatives will join up with another party to form a coalition majority government.

free market A market economy in which there is no government interference in the form of regulation or subsidy. In a free market price is governed purely by the theory of supply and demand.

free speech The concept that people have the right to say whatever they want without fear of reprisal. In practice the term also implies that people have the right to publish or broadcast in written or spoken form anything they want by any means available, such as newspapers, the radio, television and the internet. In his work *On Liberty*, John Stuart Mill argued that freedom of expression should only be withdrawn 'to prevent harm to others'. This caveat has ignited innumerable debates about individuals' rights.

laissez faire (French 'leave to do') An economic term used to describe a market that is free from government intervention. The phrase dates back to the late 17th century, but was picked up and popularized by classical economists in the mid 19th century. See also *free market*.

legislature The government body that is responsible for creating a state's or nation's legislation. Legislation is a collection of laws or enactments that impact on just about every aspect of our daily lives, from determining criminality to health and safety, from school attendance to raising taxes. The legislative body in the United States is Congress, in the United Kingdom and most European countries it is parliament.

majority faction A phrase used by political theorist James Madison in his essay Number 10 of *The Federalist* papers, in which he voiced concerns that majority rule would lead to the erosion of the rights of smaller factions and individuals. Madison argued that a large republic (by which he meant a national representative democracy) would safeguard the rights of minorities.

mixed economy A term used to describe an economy in which there are both deregulated and regulated elements. Most developed countries, while aiming for a free market in terms of the free movement of goods, labour, and so on, include some form of government intervention, whether through subsidies of railroads or airlines, or through the provision of welfare.

paternalism A political system in which government interferes with the rights of individuals against their will on the pretext of affording them protection or benefiting them in some other way. While governments argue that certain measures, such as crash-helmet and seat-belt enforcement, protect individuals from harming themselves, campaigners see them as an attack on civil liberties.

positive liberty A concept associated with liberalism in the 20th century; it promotes a more proactive government that implements policies and tackles socio-economic issues with a view to helping people achieve self-sufficiency and self-realization.

privatization The transfer of public services, agencies or assets to the private sector. Governments, whether local or national, tend to privatize either to raise revenue, cut costs or to create more cost-efficient services due to free-market competition. During the 1980s governments of both the United States and the United Kingdom privatized large swathes of nationally owned assets as part of fiscal conservatism's deregulatory ideology, while following the collapse of the Soviet Union significant state-owned enterprises were disposed of in Eastern Europe and Russia during the 1990s.

ANARCHISM

the 30-second politics

Consider this thought experiment.
Imagine a stranger, a thief, knocks on your door and demands at gunpoint that you hand over a large sum of money. Now imagine that this stranger wears a shiny silver badge that says 'government'. Does that badge somehow legitimate his demand? Further suppose that the stranger provides evidence that he was hired by a majority of people in your neighbourhood to forcibly collect money for improvements in the neighbourhood. Now are you ethically bound (as opposed to simply being frightened out of your mind) to hand over the money? If you think not, you may be more of an anarchist than you may have realized. Government entails coercion – the threat and use of force to uphold its authority and laws – and anarchists are persons who believe that there exists no legitimate warrant for government coercion. What else anarchists believe varies radically. Some anarchists believe in collective social action – provided that it is voluntary. Others believe that radically free individuals should be completely unconstrained by unwanted social constraints. And some believe that even property itself, which requires protection by force, is illegitimate. Anarchist movements have sprung up in nations all over the world from the 19th century onwards, but their appeal has always been severely limited.

RELATED THEORIES
See also
PRAETORIANISM
page 48
ANARCHO-SYNDICALISM
page 112

3-SECOND BIOGRAPHIES
PIERRE-JOSEPH PROUDHON
1809–1865
French thinker and possible originator of the name 'anarchist'

MIKHAIL A. BAKUNIN
1814–1876
Russian revolutionary who advocated collectivist anarchism

ROBERT PAUL WOLFF
1933–
Contemporary American advocate of 'philosophical anarchism'

30-SECOND TEXT
Michael E. Bailey

3-SECOND SOUNDBITE
Anarchism is less a coherent philosophy than a wildly diverse assemblage of political beliefs that converge only on being anti-authority, anti-state and anti-coercion.

3-MINUTE MANIFESTO
Proving anarchists wrong is a tricky business. The United States and United Kingdom have been profoundly influenced by social contract theory, which holds that governments derive their legitimate authority from the consent of the governed. The 18th-century philosopher David Hume mocked social contract theory, noting that very few people have ever had the opportunity to consent to (or reject) their government. Hume instead justified government's legitimacy by the fact that without government, democratic or otherwise, civilization would crumble.

'That government is best which governs not at all.'
HENRY DAVID THOREAU

REPRESENTATIVE DEMOCRACY
the 30-second politics

The most fundamental idea

behind democracy is that the people govern themselves. However, the problem is that true self-government, where the citizens actually participate in daily government, is a practical impossibility. While it is theoretically possible for very small societies to allow all of their members to participate in governance, once a society grows to the size of modern countries, such activities are impossible. Even in a country such as Iceland, which is small in terms of both geography and population (roughly 310,000 inhabitants) there are still serious barriers for effective government by all adults. Where would they all meet? How would they find the time to devote themselves to government? How could they have time for adequate debate if everyone were given even a few minutes to express their opinions? This problem becomes even more obvious in larger democracies, such as the United States (over 300 million inhabitants) or India (over one billion). As a result, modern democratic government has evolved into a system wherein the population goes to the polls to vote for politicians who are supposed to represent the interests of the voters. Those politicians are then responsible to those voters on a regular basis, as they must periodically go before the voters to ask for re-election.

3-SECOND SOUNDBITE
People tend not to have the time, interest or the knowledge needed to govern themselves, so they elect representatives to do so on their behalf.

3-MINUTE MANIFESTO
Since representative democracy requires elected representatives in lieu of all governing all, the need to organize interests and structure electoral competition becomes vital. Enter the political party: a group of individuals organized around a signalling mechanism (the party's label that gives voters some idea about its policy positions) that competes for votes in competitive elections. Further, parties would become responsible for governing once elected (especially in parliamentary systems). Parties are ubiquitous in modern representative democracies.

RELATED THEORIES
See also
DEMOCRACY
page 24
MAJORITARIANISM
page 60
PROPORTIONAL
REPRESENTATION
page 62
PARLIAMENTARY DEMOCRACY
page 92

3-SECOND BIOGRAPHIES
JAMES MADISON
1751–1836
Political theorist and primary architect of the US Constitution

JOHN STUART MILL
1806–1873
Political theorist, representative democracy supporter

30-SECOND TEXT
Steven L. Taylor

'The right of voting for representatives is the primary right by which other rights are protected.'

THOMAS PAINE

MAJORITARIANISM

the 30-second politics

On the surface, the concept of majoritarianism is immensely appealing because it reflects the fundamental value behind democracy; if a majority of the people want something, it is reasonable to suggest that the government then ought to do that thing. However, majoritarian values often come into conflict with the belief that the rights of political, religious or ethnic minorities should be protected. One of the best-known statements of this concern is James Madison's *The Federalist* Number 10, in which he argues that 'majority faction' is the most dangerous threat to the long-term health of representative democracy. For example, the experience of African-Americans in the post-Civil War United States, particularly in the South, amply illustrates what can happen if a majority is determined to relegate a minority to second-class citizenship. Nonetheless the core appeal of majoritarianism remains intact and is often invoked, at least by the side having the majority's support in an argument, as a morally persuasive basis for why its position should carry the day.

3-SECOND SOUNDBITE
The government should adopt the position of the majority of the people on any given issue.

3-MINUTE MANIFESTO
Majoritarianism can be problematic because the public often holds opinions that are contradictory. For example, citizens in many democratic countries believe in the value of free speech in the abstract but would deny it to disfavoured and extremist groups; in Europe, for instance, some countries forbid pro-Nazi or pro-communist political organizations. A majority of citizens may also espouse ideas that are politically or economically impracticable, such as simultaneously believing that taxes should be lowered and government spending should be increased.

RELATED THEORIES
See also
DEMOCRACY
page 24
POPULAR SOVEREIGNTY
page 26
REPRESENTATIVE DEMOCRACY
page 58

3-SECOND BIOGRAPHIES
ALEXIS DE TOCQUEVILLE
1805–1859
French aristocrat who defined the 'tyranny of the majority'

STEPHEN A. DOUGLAS
1813–1861
US senator who proposed that new states should determine whether to be 'free' or 'slave' states by popular vote

30-SECOND TEXT
Christopher N. Lawrence

'Decision by majorities is as much an expedient as lighting by gas.'
WILLIAM EWART GLADSTONE

PROPORTIONAL REPRESENTATION

the 30-second politics

3-SECOND SOUNDBITE
Political parties receive roughly the same percentage of seats in the legislature as they received in votes in the election.

3-MINUTE MANIFESTO
The main debate over the use of PR is one of representation versus fragmentation/stability. The more proportional an electoral system is, the more likely it is that various political interests will be represented in the national legislature. Of course, the more interests that are represented will likely mean an increase in the number of parties in the legislature. More parties mean that coalition formation to pass legislation (or to form the government in a parliamentary democracy) becomes more difficult.

When it comes to electing

politicians to serve in government, there are two broad types of electoral systems that can be used. One is a majoritarian system, such as is used in the United States and United Kingdom, where individual candidates compete in a district to win a single seat. Another is a proportional representation (PR) system in which parties compete in multi-member districts, that is, more than one legislator will be elected from that district. In PR systems the foundational notion is that each party will receive roughly the same percentage of seats in the legislature as it won in votes across the country – in other words, if Party X received 20 per cent of the vote it would receive 20 per cent of the seats. In reality most PR systems do not perfectly allocate seats in this manner, but tend to come relatively close. There are a variety of factors that come into play to determine exactly how proportional a system will be, such as the exact method of translating votes into seats, the number of seats contested per district, as well as other structural and legal factors. PR systems typically require that parties submit lists of candidates to compete in districts, although some systems instead allow multiple candidates per party.

RELATED THEORIES
See also
DEMOCRACY
page 24
REPRESENTATIVE DEMOCRACY
page 58
MAJORITARIANISM
page 60
PARLIAMENTARY DEMOCRACY
page 92

3-SECOND BIOGRAPHIES
MAURICE DUVERGER
1917–
French political scientist/theorist

MATTHEW S. SHUGART
1960–
US theorist/professor

30-SECOND TEXT
Steven L. Taylor

'... the first principle of democracy [is] representation in proportion to numbers.'
JOHN STUART MILL

CLASSICAL LIBERALISM

the 30-second politics

3-SECOND SOUNDBITE
Individual liberty and
the pursuit of fortune
predominate in this 18th-
and 19th-century ideology,
which holds that the
government that governs
least governs best.

3-MINUTE MANIFESTO
A curiosity of classical
liberalism is its tangle of
views about human
capability. In the classical
liberal world, individuals
who are perfectly wise in
their pursuit of economic
gain (inviolably so)
immediately become
altogether foolish when
they pool their efforts to
reform society through
politics. And paternalism,
which is utterly abhorrent
from government officials,
was not only accepted but
embraced as necessary
when at the direction of
the barons of industry.

Power versus liberty. Government
versus the individual. At the heart of classical
liberalism, a political philosophy that began to
emerge in England, France and the United
States in the late 18th century, is a commitment
to limiting government power so that individuals
may pursue their own economic self-interest
freely. Classical liberalism borrowed from the
English and American 18th-century political
devotion to individual rights, the rule of law,
separation of powers and checks and balances,
while adding a new commitment to laissez faire
economics. Some classical liberals were deeply
pessimistic about the future prospects
for society, while for others social progress
became an article of faith; but for both
pessimists and optimists alike, any good in
society is jeopardized by excessive government
meddling. Like a teacher who trains his
students into helplessness by always providing
them with the answers, paternalist efforts of
the government to assist people – that is, going
beyond its traditional role of protecting property
and establishing order – ends up hurting its
intended beneficiaries. Early on in England, and
later in the United States, the tenets of classical
liberalism were employed to rationalize as a
necessary evil the suffering and misery
associated with industrialization.

RELATED THEORIES
See also
LIBERALISM
page 70

LIBERTARIANISM
page 72

CAPITALISM
page 118

3-SECOND BIOGRAPHIES
ADAM SMITH
1723–1790
Scottish economist who called
for free trade

HERBERT SPENCER
1820–1903
English philosopher, advocate of
economic 'survival of the fittest'

30-SECOND TEXT
Michael E. Bailey

'We hold these truths to
be self-evident, that all
men are created equal,
that they are endowed
by their Creator with
certain unalienable
rights, that among these
are life, liberty and the
pursuit of happiness.'
THOMAS JEFFERSON

1632
Born, Somerset, UK

1652
Attended Oxford
University

1667
Employed in the
household of Lord
Cooper 1st Earl of
Shaftesbury

1675
Travelled through France

1679
Returned to England;
composed most of *Two
Treatises of Government*

1689
*An Essay Concerning
Human Understanding*
first published

1690
*Two Treatises of
Government* first
published

1693
Tract entitled *Some
Thoughts Concerning
Education* published

1704
Died, Essex, UK

JOHN LOCKE

Of the many celebrated figures of the Enlightenment, few if any can claim to have made such an impact on modern political thinking as John Locke. Locke was among the first to question the concept of absolute authority and to examine the relationship between the individual and the State.

In 1647, aged 15, Locke attended Westminster School in London, before going on to Oxford University in 1652, where – along with a somewhat sterile classical education – he also studied medicine, and was introduced to the works of the exciting new modern philosophers, notably René Descartes. Descartes' philosophy of ideas was to set Locke on his own path to empiricism, in which he argued that we are not born with innate knowledge, but rather as blank slates (*tabula rasa*) and that our knowledge is gained over time through experience and perception – ideas fully expressed in his philosophical work *An Essay Concerning Human Understanding*, published in 1690.

While at Oxford John Locke made the acquaintance of Lord Cooper, 1st Earl of Shaftesbury and Chancellor of the Exchequer. Although Shaftesbury's personal physician, it was as secretary to Shaftesbury's newly formed Board of Trade and Plantations that Locke developed an appreciation of international trade and commerce, and a taste for economics and politics in general.

However, it was in his *Two Treatises of Government*, first published in 1689, that Locke set out his political stance. The first treatise is an attack on the divine right of kings and absolute monarchy. In the second treatise Locke argues the case for benign governance based on the concept of a 'social contract' – in exchange for relinquishing certain rights to the State, men can expect to be protected, governed fairly and be allowed to pursue their natural rights of 'life, liberty, health and property'. It was a political theory that was to lead to classical liberalism and which later was to resonate so powerfully in the *Declaration of Independence*.

CONSERVATISM

the 30-second politics

Conservatism cannot be distilled into a set of policies, and the causes that conservatives have championed vary dramatically from era to era and from one nation to another. Turn the pages of a history book and eventually you will encounter both libertarian and big-state conservatives, internationalist and isolationist conservatives, conservatives who are both democratic and aristocratic, and those who are both technophile as well as technophobe. What holds conservatism together as a coherent approach to politics is a family of beliefs and attitudes about human beings and society. Most conservatives firmly believe that human beings possess a fixed nature that impedes all political efforts to remake society from scratch. Try as they may, political revolutionaries and even do-gooder government 'experts' inevitably fall short – often at the expense of lives and individual liberty – when they seek to bring their Utopian blueprints to life. Conservatives believe that decent and liveable civilizations are difficult to establish and maddeningly fragile. Preserving society requires that government and society establish law and order, acknowledge that inequality of talent and authority is inevitable, promote religion and the teaching of virtue, defend the worth of family and traditional social groups and unapologetically encourage the patriotic love of country.

3-SECOND SOUNDBITE
Conservatism is a political and social philosophy that embraces traditional values and institutions, holding that society moves forward best while looking backward.

3-MINUTE MANIFESTO
Conservatives sometimes celebrate the efforts of *past* reformers – once those reformers have left the political arena to ride off into the sunset. Today's progressive liberals or reformers can become tomorrow's conservative heroes if their innovations prove beneficial. In the American and British context, yesterday's conservatives resisted the expansion of suffrage to those without property and to women and minorities but today point to universal suffrage as a sign of conservative justice and commitment to democracy.

RELATED THEORIES
See also
CLASSICAL LIBERALISM
page 64
NEOCONSERVATISM
page 144

3-SECOND BIOGRAPHIES
EDMUND BURKE
1729–1797
Widely recognized as 'the father of conservatism'

RONALD REAGAN
1911–2004
Iconic conservative US president

MARGARET THATCHER
1925
Influential conservative British prime minster

30-SECOND TEXT
Michael E. Bailey

'What is conservatism? Is it not adherence to the old and tried, against the new and untried?'
ABRAHAM LINCOLN

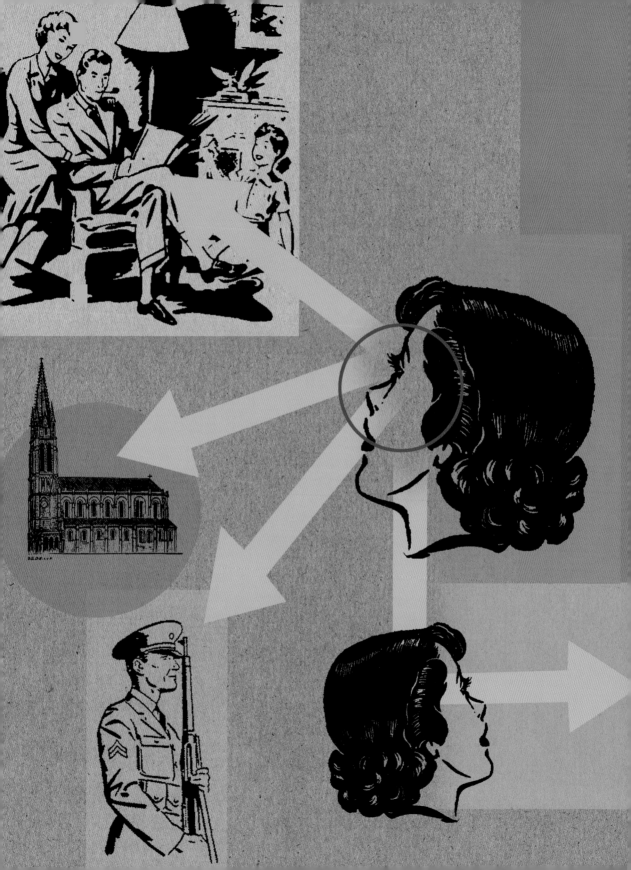

LIBERALISM

the 30-second politics

Liberalism is the political doctrine of individual liberation, security from harm and equal rights. These three traits, seemingly a harmonious triangle of compatible ideas, actually exist in deep tension with one another, and liberal thought perennially struggles with how to properly weight each of these values. In its 18th-century manifestations, such as in the early years of the American republic, liberalism placed individual liberty as the top priority, de-emphasizing equality of rights or protection from harm except for direct rights violations. In the 20th century, however, liberals began to note that meaningful liberty cannot be separated from security or equal access to government. Liberals began to promote the idea of positive liberty, which through a variety of programmes such as public education, aims at equipping citizens with the skills to increase their opportunities for meaningful life choices. Well-designed government regulations could lead to greater individual liberty by ensuring greater security, such as when the government insures individual bank deposits. Liberals also began to emphasize the interconnectedness of society, noting how harm can result to individuals when economic systems such as capitalism lead to massive inequality, poverty and squalor, and dangerous work conditions.

3-SECOND SOUNDBITE
People are born free and equal, and it's government's job to keep them that way.

3-MINUTE MANIFESTO
The good news is that people are born free and equal, and owners of their own lives. The bad news is that people's liberty and equality – indeed their overall wellbeing – is forever threatened not only by human beings but by natural catastrophes, pollution, and economic products and social systems. Providing security to individuals requires regulation over ever increasing swathes of social life. Thus as modern government protects individuals, it leaves them isolated and politically impotent.

RELATED THEORIES
See also
CLASSICAL LIBERALISM
page 64
KEYNESIANISM
page 124
NEOLIBERALISM
page 128

3-SECOND BIOGRAPHIES
FRANKLIN D. ROOSEVELT
1882–1945
US president and advocate of the welfare state

JOHN MAYNARD KEYNES
1883–1946
English economist

JOHN RAWLS
1921–2002
US political philosopher

30-SECOND TEXT
Michael E. Bailey

'We have come to a clear realization of the fact that true individual freedom cannot exist without economic security and indepen-dence. "Necessitous men are not free men".'
FRANKLIN D. ROOSEVELT

LIBERTARIANISM

the 30-second politics

Imagine a stranger approaches you on the street and expresses a desire to dramatically improve your life. You demurely decline his assistance, but the stranger persists, insisting he can help you with your finances, the quality of your children's education, the safety of your workplace and even in your spiritual life. In short, you perceive this person as a threat, and you stand bewildered as to why he believes he can order your affairs better than yourself. Libertarians view expansive government, no matter how well-intended, just as we view this stranger – as an assault on individual integrity and liberty. Libertarians are not anarchists, they believe that government has a necessary and important, if quite limited, function. Though no two libertarians think exactly alike – that's part of the beauty of libertarianism – virtually all libertarians believe that government should be strictly restricted to preventing, and punishing, citizens from harming one another in their liberty, their property and their lives. In short, government's purpose is to protect people's rights. Modern-day libertarianism has a strong free market-economic component, as libertarians believe that society flourishes when individuals following their own self-interest are allowed to enter into contracts with other free individuals.

RELATED THEORIES
See also
CLASSICAL LIBERALISM
page 64
CONSERVATISM
page 68
CAPITALISM
page 118

3-SECOND BIOGRAPHIES
JOHN STUART MILL
1806–1873
Major British philosopher who sought to maximize individual social liberty

FRIEDRICH HAYEK
1899–1992
Influential Austrian economist who criticized state intervention

MILTON FRIEDMAN
1912–2006
Highly influential US economist

30-SECOND TEXT
Michael E. Bailey

3-SECOND SOUNDBITE
Libertarianism is the political creed of less is more – or, governing best by governing very little.

3-MINUTE MANIFESTO
The libertarian understanding of liberty is essentially 'being left alone' – free, for example, to say whatever and pray however you wish. But being left alone does not always give one a meaningful choice. My freedom to swim ashore is meaningless if I am on a boat in the middle of an ocean. Critics of libertarians argue that *positive* freedom – the capacity to fulfil one's full potential – requires government programmes including public education, universal health care and protection from environmental degradation.

'Giving money and power to government is like giving whisky and car keys to teenage boys.'

P.J. O'ROURKE

SOCIAL DEMOCRACY

the 30-second politics

A social democracy is one that combines the ideas of representative democracy with a partially or wholly socialist economic order, where key sectors (if not the entirety) of the economy are controlled directly or indirectly by the State. After the Second World War, social democracy was widely adopted in Western Europe (and, to a lesser extent, other advanced industrial democracies such as Canada and Japan). It was seen as a compromise between the capitalist representative democracies that existed in the United States and prewar Europe and the communist authoritarian and totalitarian regimes established during the same period in Eastern Europe and China. Many of these countries adopted a 'welfare state' that provided for basic material and health needs for all citizens, while at the same time either nationalizing or otherwise highly regulating those major economic activities such as transportation, banking, industrial production and mining that were traditionally part of the private sector. By the middle of the 1970s, however, many of these countries' governments found that their high degree of involvement in the economy had undermined the competitiveness of their industries and national economic growth, and began a process of privatization to reduce state ownership of the economy.

3-SECOND SOUNDBITE
Social democracy sees a strong role for the State in redistributing income and owning industry.

3-MINUTE MANIFESTO
Most contemporary representative democracies have a 'mixed' economy with the State playing a key role in at least some sectors of the economy, but to a lesser extent than was envisaged by advocates of full social democracy. The main differences today between 'capitalist' democracies such as the United States and 'social' democracies such as Sweden lie in the degree to which the government is involved in economic redistribution, the generosity of the government's 'safety net' and ownership of key economic agents.

RELATED THEORIES
See also
DEMOCRACY
page 24
COMMUNISM
page 102
SOCIALISM
page 120

3-SECOND BIOGRAPHIES
EDUARD BERNSTEIN
1850–1932
German critic of Karl Marx, the 'father' of social democracy

WILLIAM BEVERIDGE
1879–1963
English economist; author of the 'Beveridge Report'

30-SECOND TEXT
Christopher N. Lawrence

'Democracy is indispensable to socialism.'
VLADIMIR LENIN

ELEMENTS OF DEMOCRACY

ELEMENTS OF DEMOCRACY
GLOSSARY

cabinet A collection of senior government representatives. In a parliamentary system the cabinet is composed of members of the legislature and is collectively and individually responsible to the legislature. The cabinet makes collective policy decisions, while individual members, known as ministers, are responsible for specific key political portfolios, such as health, education or transport for example. In most presidential systems, however, members of the cabinet provide a more advisory role and are not allowed to sit on the legislature.

canton A political or administrative subdivision of a country. Cantons tend to be smaller in size and population than other political or administrative subdivisions, such as states or provinces.

head of state A country's principal public representative. The role of the head of state depends on a country's specific constitution. The monarch of a constitutional monarchy, for example, although head of state, primarily performs ceremonial duties only, as does the president of most parliamentary republics. In most presidential systems, however, the president is the head of government as well as the head of state and will have specific executive powers.

loss of confidence In a parliamentary system, the opposition can express a loss of confidence in the government by putting forward a motion of no confidence. If parliament subsequently votes for the motion, the government must either resign or call a general election.

parliamentary government A system of government in which executive power is exercised by selected members of the legislature (parliament) who form a group or cabinet of ministers that is accountable to parliament. Parliamentary systems tend to be more collective in nature compared with presidential systems; however critics point to the lack of separation between the executive and legislative powers.

prerogative power The power of the head of state to act outside established law. The term is derived from the feudal English royal prerogative, in which the monarch had an 'undefined residue of power which he might use for the public good'. Then and today, an executive's primary use of prerogative power centres around reacting to the threat of war.

presidential government A system of government in which the entire executive power is vested in the president and kept separate from legislative and judicial powers. The president is not accountable to the legislature, and while the president does not propose bills, he or she has the power to veto them. The president, unlike the head of government in a parliamentary system, is elected directly by the people for a fixed term.

prime minister The name given to the head of government in some parliamentary systems; the term is synonymous with premier. Unlike a president, a prime minister is not the head of state, a role which in most parliamentary systems is only ceremonial. Furthermore a prime minister is not elected directly by the people, instead the post falls to the leader of whichever political party is voted into power during nationwide general elections.

LEGISLATIVE POWER

the 30-second politics

Legislative power is, most fundamentally, the power to establish, modify and abolish laws and other rules that are used to govern a society. Most people associate the legislative power with parliaments and other representative assemblies, which are often referred to as legislatures, but in practice national constitutions and laws may delegate some aspects of law-making authority to the executive branch of government – for example, by vesting the president with the power to make decrees or executive orders, or giving a prime minister the authority to advise the monarch to exercise their 'reserve' or 'prerogative' powers. While the legislature typically has the broadest authority to make laws (and in theory, in a parliamentary democracy, that power is unlimited), nonetheless regulations, orders in council, statutory instruments and similar rules made by bureaucrats, presidents and prime ministers can carry the same legal force as a law. Court orders can also, at times, have the effect of making law, rather than just interpreting it. The legislative power may even be exercised by the people directly, by voting in a referendum or when meeting as a legislative body themselves.

3-SECOND SOUNDBITE
A government's authority to establish laws and other rules.

3-MINUTE MANIFESTO
Even where there is a clear design involving the separation of powers, introducing checks and balances can give executive-branch officials an important law-making role. For example, in the United States, the presidential veto allows presidents to reject legislation proposed by Congress. Meanwhile the vice president is both an executive-branch official and the presiding officer of the Senate, albeit with limited powers in practice today.

RELATED THEORIES
See also
EXECUTIVE POWER
page 82
SEPARATION OF POWERS
page 86
CHECKS AND BALANCES
page 90
PARLIAMENTARY DEMOCRACY
page 92

3-SECOND BIOGRAPHIES
HENRY III
1207–1272
First English monarch to summon a parliament to raise taxes

JOSEPH G. CANNON
1836–1926
Speaker of the US House of Representatives, famous for his control over the chamber

30-SECOND TEXT
Christopher N. Lawrence

'Laws, like sausages, cease to inspire respect in proportion as we know how they are made.'
JOHN GODREY SAXE

EXECUTIVE POWER

the 30-second politics

Executive power is the key
element distinguishing governmental power from
other kinds of authority. Churches, schools and
corporations are all free (in free societies) to
make whatever claims they want about society
(or the universe, for that matter), but these
pronouncements mean very little without
the power to back them up. What makes
government *government* is the power of
coercion – the power to make people behave
in an involuntary manner through the threat of
loss of liberty or money or even death – and it
is the executive branch that holds this power. It is
the force that runs the day-to-day administration
of government and which carries out the laws,
keeps order and fights wars. It is also the power
that gives government its capacity both to do
great good and terrible harm. Without executive
enforcement, even legislative and judicial powers
are mere suggestions. After the US Supreme
Court declared in 1954 that racial segregation in
schools was unconstitutional, for years southern
segregated schools did absolutely nothing to
comply with the Court's ruling. Only when
Congress pushed the executive power to force
the issue did schools begin to act, and within a
few years, the vast majority of southern schools
were undergoing desegregation.

3-SECOND SOUNDBITE
The power to carry out the
law, and then some.

3-MINUTE MANIFESTO
Executive power originated
in monarchy, and one of
the most controversial
legacies of monarchical
power is prerogative
power, the power for
executives to act for the
national good in the
absence of, or even
contrary to, established
law – for example through
sending troops into action
without authorization
from the formal
war-declaring institution
of government. How to
'tame' this useful but
dangerous power is a
perennial constitutional
challenge that may never
be fully resolved.

RELATED THEORIES
See also
MONARCHY
page 14
DESPOTISM
page 16
LEGISLATIVE POWER
page 80

3-SECOND BIOGRAPHIES
NICCOLO MACHIAVELLI
1469–1527
Italian political philosopher who
addressed the prince's need to
be feared rather than loved

JOHN LOCKE
1632–1704
see pages 66–7

ALEXANDER HAMILTON
1757–1804
US constitutional thinker
and supporter of strong
executive power

30-SECOND TEXT
Michael E. Bailey

'The President is at
liberty, both in law and
conscience, to be as
big a man as he can.'
WOODROW WILSON

JUDICIAL POWER

the 30-second politics

Judicial power is the authority
to decide the guilt (or liability) of an alleged
lawbreaker, as well as the punishment that will
be applied if found responsible. For much of
human history, judicial and executive powers
were fused; a ruler who believed someone was
guilty of a crime would also punish the offender.
Over time, however, as societies became more
populous, a separation of these powers emerged
in practice, since kings and queens had more
important things to do with their time than
arbitrating the petty disputes of their subjects.
In most countries, judges (either alone, or in
conjunction with a jury) are responsible for
interpreting the laws in force and applying
them to the specific circumstances in question.
Judges may also investigate crimes themselves,
particularly in countries with laws based on
the Napoleonic Code, such as France or Italy; in
most English-speaking countries, investigations
are typically the responsibility of the executive
branch or another independent authority.
Judicial power extends both to disputes
between citizens (or between groups such as
corporations) where the State serves as arbiter
– issues of civil law – and to situations where
a citizen or group is accused of an offence
against the state – issues of criminal law.

3-SECOND SOUNDBITE
The authority to
interpret and apply
laws in specific cases.

3-MINUTE MANIFESTO
Historically legislatures
also had the power to
punish alleged criminals by
passing what were known
as bills of attainder, which
punished a named person
or group of people without
trial or other recourse
(save, perhaps, for a
pardon from the monarch
or other chief executive).
Democracies today either
do not have the power to
pass bills of attainder or
refrain from doing so.

RELATED THEORIES
See also
LEGISLATIVE POWER
page 80

EXECUTIVE POWER
page 82

SEPARATION OF POWERS
page 86

CHECKS AND BALANCES
page 90

3-SECOND BIOGRAPHIES
JOHN MARSHALL
(1755–1835)
Chief Justice of the US Supreme
Court who helped establish the
principle of judicial review

OLIVER WENDELL
HOLMES JR.
(1841–1935)
Noted jurist and former Justice
of the US Supreme Court

30-SECOND TEXT
Christopher N. Lawrence

'The judiciary is
the safeguard of
our liberty and our
property under the
Constitution.'
CHARLES E. HUGHES

SEPARATION OF POWERS

the 30-second politics

Separation of powers is a model
for distributing governmental power within a
democracy that emphasizes placing the legislative
(law-making), executive (law-implementing) and
judicial (law-applying) functions in distinct hands.
It is often contrasted with parliamentary systems,
which marry the legislative and executive
functions in the prime minister's cabinet. One of
the underlying ideas of separation of powers –
and one that is taken as an article of faith in the
United States – is that concentrated political
power is a threat to individual liberty. If the police
who *execute* the law are free to make up rules
(that is, act *legislatively*), and issue punishments
on the spot (that is, act *judicially*), what would
prevent them from behaving badly? Only their
consciences – a thought that mortified such
pessimists as Montesquieu and James Madison.
In the US context, it was not concern for
individual rights that led to the federal separation
of powers system. Instead, the three separate
branches were designed to strengthen, not
weaken, the federal government. Presidential
governments, as opposed to parliamentary ones,
most closely fit a pure model of separation of
powers, though many nations around the world
separate their branches, especially the judicial
branch, at least to some degree.

3-SECOND SOUNDBITE
The legislative, executive
and judicial *functions*
are lodged in three
distinct and independent
institutions – keep them
separated.

3-MINUTE MANIFESTO
Separation of powers is not
a simple, or perhaps even
a single, idea – and, in
fact, political conflict and
tension is built into the
system like a coil. Political
scientists disagree on *what*
exactly needs separating,
the *degree* to which it
should be separated and
the *effects* of separation.
Woodrow Wilson even took
the view that the president,
the chief *executive*, ought
to be a *legislative* leader. In
his view, the Constitution
created independent
political institutions,
but the functions of
government – legislative,
executive and judicial –
are shared between them.

RELATED THEORIES
See also
LEGISLATIVE POWER
page 80
EXECUTIVE POWER
page 82
JUDICIAL POWER
page 84

3-SECOND BIOGRAPHIES
JOHN LOCKE
1632–1704
see pages 66–7

BARON DE MONTESQUIEU
1689–1795
see pages 88–9

JAMES MADISON
1751–1836
Important architect of the US
Constitution and 4th president

30-SECOND TEXT
Michael E. Bailey

*'The accumulation of
all powers ... in the same
hands, whether of one, a
few, or many, and whether
hereditary, self-appointed,
or elective, may justly
be pronounced the very
definition of tyranny.'*
JAMES MADISON

1689
Born, La Brède, France

1705
Studied law in Bordeaux

1715
Married Jeanne de
Latrigue

1716
Inherited the title of
Baron de La Brède et de
Montesquieu and the role
of *président à mortier*
from his uncle

1721
Published *Persian Letters*

1728
Left France in order to
travel abroad

1730
Elected to the Royal
Society in London

1732
Returned to France

1748
Published *The Spirit of
the Laws*

1755
Died, Bordeaux

CHARLES-LOUIS DE SECONDAT, BARON DE MONTESQUIEU

A man of the Enlightenment, whose satirical impressions of Parisian society were acutely observed, Charles-Louis de Secondat, Baron de Montesquieu will be remembered best as a hugely influential political philosopher.

Montesquieu was born in 1689 at La Brède, near Bordeaux, France. He studied and worked as a legal councillor before inheriting in 1716 from his uncle the title Baron de La Brède et de Montesquieu and the legal role of *président à mortier* in the Bordeaux Parlement, a form of appeal court.

In 1721 Montesquieu published *Persian Letters*, the first of his two most notable works. Written in the form of a series of letters recounting the experiences of two Persian noblemen journeying from Isfahan to Paris, the work is both a biting satire on the mores and fashions of contemporary Paris and a more sober reflection on the role of government, religion, law and the nature of power.

In 1725 Montesquieu gave up the post of *président à mortier* and following his election to the Académie Française in 1728, embarked on a tour of Hungary, Turkey, Germany and England, specifically to observe their legal, social and governmental institutions.

He returned to France in 1732 and began his most celebrated work *The Spirit of the Laws*. Published in 1748, the treatise is a work of political, social and legal anthropology and philosophy. Of greatest significance are Montesquieu's theories on government. He asserts there are three types: monarchical, despotic and republican government. The first governs under a sense of honour, the second by fear and the third, by a constitution. Furthermore, in order to stop any abuse of power he argued for the separation of the executive, the legislature (which should, he proposed, be made up of two houses) and the judiciary – this 'separation of powers' is a cornerstone of the US Constitution.

CHECKS AND BALANCES

the 30-second politics

When you are vaccinated, a touch of a disease-causing agent is introduced into your bloodstream so your body can better develop an immunity against that disease. It's a strategy of fighting biological fire with fire, so to speak. Similarly, checks and balances constitutionally fights fire with fire by requiring the three branches of government – Congress, president and the courts (in the context of the United States) – to share with each other some of their respective powers (legislative, executive and judicial). James Madison, 18th-century US constitutional thinker, put it this way: 'Ambition must be made to counteract ambition'. When a checks and balances scheme is functioning as intended, the independence of each branch is preserved. Consequently, checks and balances is not to be confused with parliamentary systems – which fuse executive and legislative powers – but is a strategy of separation of powers. Checks and balances is not uniquely American, but it is exemplified in the US system; examples of checks abound within the Constitution. One example is the veto, which gives the president, the chief *executive*, a lot of *legislative* influence. Likewise, even though military affairs are traditionally the domain of a nation's chief executive, the US Constitution grants Congress the power to declare war.

3-SECOND SOUNDBITE
Checks and balances joins together (at least a little) what separation of powers has put asunder.

3-MINUTE MANIFESTO
By requiring agreement between branches to get things done (for example, both the president and Senate must agree to treaties), checks and balances can often generate conflict between the branches. When conflict between the branches is so protracted it prevents government from doing its work, we call that gridlock. All constitutional democracies must decide whether to emphasize effective majority rule, as typical of parliamentary systems, or whether to limit the powers of government, as typical of checks and balances.

RELATED THEORIES
See also
SEPARATION OF POWERS
page 86
PARLIAMENTARY DEMOCRACY
page 92

3-SECOND BIOGRAPHIES
BARON DE MONTESQUIEU
1689–1795
see pages 88–9

JAMES MADISON
1751–1836
Important architect of the US Constitution and 4th president

JOHN MARSHALL
1755–1835
US Supreme Court chief justice who established the Court's power to strike down laws as unconstitutional

30-SECOND TEXT
Michael E. Bailey

'If men were angels, no government would be necessary. If angels were to govern men, neither external nor internal controls on government would be necessary.'
JAMES MADISON

PARLIAMENTARY DEMOCRACY

the 30-second politics

3-SECOND SOUNDBITE
A system in which the voters elect the legislature and the legislature creates the executive.

3-MINUTE MANIFESTO
The electoral calendar in a parliamentary system is not fixed, meaning that while there is a maximum number of years that are allowed to pass between elections, it is also possible for early elections to be called either because of the aforementioned loss of confidence (see page 78) or because the dominant party leadership believes that new elections would have the chance of enhancing the size of a governing majority (as well as extending their time in office).

Parliamentary democracy is a system of fused powers in which the voters elect the legislature and the legislature (frequently called the parliament) elects the executive (known as the government or the cabinet). This is to be contrasted with a separation-of-powers (such as a presidential) system in which the voters independently elect the legislature and the executive. Typically, the head of a government in a parliamentary system is called the prime minister and the members of the cabinet are called ministers. Ministers in a parliamentary system are all normally members of the legislature unlike in presidential systems where it is typically the case that members of the cabinet cannot be members of the legislature. The prime minister and the cabinet serve as long as they can maintain the confidence of a majority of legislators. Should that confidence be lost, a new cabinet must be formed – an action that may require new elections. The creation and maintenance of such majorities gets more complicated the more parties that are in the legislature. The head of state in a parliamentary system is not the prime minister, but rather is either a constitutional monarch (such as in the United Kingdom and Spain) or is vested in an appointed president or other official (as in Germany and Israel).

RELATED THEORIES
See also
DEMOCRACY
page 24
LEGISLATIVE POWER
page 80
EXECUTIVE POWER
page 82
SEPARATION OF POWERS
page 86

3-SECOND BIOGRAPHIES
WALTER BAGEHOT
1826–1877
British essayist

AREND LIJPHART
1936–
Professor Emeritus, University of California, San Diego

30-SECOND TEXT
Steven L. Taylor

'No government can long be secure without a formidable opposition.'
BENJAMIN DISRAELI

FEDERALISM

the 30-second politics

Federalism is a system of governing a territory in which there is a division of policy authority between the central government located in the capital and the subdivisions of a country (for which there are various terms such as states, cantons and provinces). While the ultimate power to govern the country as a whole remains with the central government (such as the power to control the monetary system or to engage in matters of foreign relations), some substantial amount of policy autonomy belongs to the sub-units (such as the creation and maintenance of schools or elements of criminal justice). Federalism is more likely to occur in territorially large countries, including Australia, Brazil, Canada, India and the United States, or in countries with internal divisions (for example differing languages) which are also linked territorially, such as Belgium and Switzerland. A key measure of exactly how much authority the sub-unit has is the amount of overall national revenue that the sub-unit controls vis-à-vis the central government. Federalism is to be contrasted with a unitary state, wherein all the policy-making authority belongs to the central government, and a confederal system, wherein the sub-units control the central government.

RELATED THEORIES
See also
REPRESENTATIVE DEMOCRACY
page 58
UNITARY STATE
page 96

3-SECOND SOUNDBITE
Federalism divides policy-making authority between a national government and its territorial subdivisions with each level having control within its given policy sphere.

3-MINUTE MANIFESTO
Federalism was arguably invented via political compromise reached at the Philadelphia Constitutional Convention of 1787. The 13 states had been functioning under the first US constitution (known as the Articles of Confederation) since independence from Great Britain and it was not working well because the states had too much power and central government had very little. The compromise was a system under which certain powers would be given to the central government while others would be retained by the states.

3-SECOND BIOGRAPHIES
WILLIAM H. RIKER
1920–1993
US political scientist and theorist

DANIEL J. ELAZAR
1934–1999
US political scientist and theorist

ALFRED STEPAN
1937–
Professor of Political Science, Columbia University

30-SECOND TEXT
Steven L. Taylor

'[Federalism should] provide for the energetic pursuit of common ends while maintaining the respective integrities of all parties.'
DANIEL J. ELAZAR

UNITARY STATE

the 30-second politics

A unitary system is one in which the central government holds all power over regional governments, though it can delegate authority to them – as well as modifying or taking it away entirely – if it chooses. The central government is generally physically located in the capital, and becomes the main symbol of political power in the country. Even when regional governments have the authority to pass and execute laws, that power lasts only as long as the central government allows. So, for example, the government of the United Kingdom grants autonomy to Scotland, Wales and Northern Ireland, but can also revoke it (and, in fact, the central government has done so periodically). A majority of countries – over 70 per cent – in the world have unitary systems. A key perceived benefit is that lines of political authority are very clear, without the confusion that may arise when different levels of government have overlapping and contested functions. In addition, in theory a unitary system removes or at least greatly reduces conflicting loyalties corresponding to local governments, though of course it does not eliminate already existing national identities (as in the UK case).

3-SECOND SOUNDBITE
Central government has all the power to giveth and taketh away from regional governments.

3-MINUTE MANIFESTO
Unitary states stand in contrast to federal systems, where state governments have extensive powers of their own that cannot be revoked by central government. The two levels of government often jealously clash over their relative authority, but both have independent prerogatives.

RELATED THEORIES
See also
FEDERALISM
page 94

3-SECOND BIOGRAPHIES
WILLIAM H. RIKER
1920–1993
US political scientist who studied the history of federalism

DANIEL ELAZAR
1934–1999
US political scientist and theorist who specialized in federalism

30-SECOND TEXT
Gregory Weeks

'*[The] crisis of the unitary state [has] encouraged the rebirth of a confusedly patriotic ideology.*'
ANTONIO GRAMSCI

COMMUNISM

COMMUNISM
GLOSSARY

bourgeoisie A term most often associated with Marxism to describe the owners of the means of production, by which is meant the capitalist upper and middle classes. Central to Marxist theory is the exploitation of the proletariat by the bourgeoisie resulting in revolution and the creation of a classless society.

Cultural Revolution A decade-long, violent ideological campaign instigated in 1966 by Mao Zedong in the People's Republic of China. Initially the campaign sought to expose elitist and liberal figures (and Mao's political enemies) in the Chinese Communist Party, and quickly spread to become a nationwide campaign to reinvigorate revolutionary zeal and suppress all intellectual and bourgeois elements. Schools were closed, millions of educated people were sent to labour camps and tens of thousands executed at the hands of the Red Guard.

Great Leap Forward A vast economic program put in place by Mao Zedong in 1958 in a bid to modernize China's agricultural and industrial base. Based on nationwide collectivization, tens of thousands of communes each comprising some 5000 families were set up and given targets to produce steel and grain. The speed of the programme, an inexperienced workforce and the massive social upheaval resulted in poor-quality manufacturing; adverse weather contributed to poor crop yields in 1959 and 1960, and by the end of the programme in 1961 some 40 million people had died of starvation.

Khmer Rouge A radical communist faction that, under the command of Pol Pot, seized control of Cambodia in 1975 and formed the Kampuchean People's Republic. The aim of the Khmer Rouge was to create a completely agrarian economy. The country was isolated from all external contact, people were forced from the cities to work on collective farms, families were separated and intellectuals and educated classes were tortured and executed. By the fall of the regime in 1978 some two million people had died through imprisonment, exhaustion and starvation.

proletariat A term used in Marxist theory to describe the working class; the proletariat do not own the means of production and therefore have to sell their labour to survive. In Marxist theory, spontaneous proletariat revolution would occur due to bourgeoisie exploitation, however Vladimir Lenin identified that imperialist colony exploitation enabled the bourgeoisie to provide domestic workers with a sufficiently high standard of living to prevent revolution. Lenin proposed that professional, dedicated revolutionaries would have to lead the proletariat to revolution for it to occur.

proletariat dictatorship In Marxism-Leninism theory, the period shortly after revolution during which the proletariat would have absolute power to completely dismantle the capitalist system, suppress any opposition and redistribute the means of production. The dictatorship of the proletariat would then be in a position to give way to a communist society.

revolutionary consciousness An awareness of and belief in the possibility and potential benefits of revolution. In Marxism-Leninism theory, for revolution to occur the proletariat would have to be educated about the immorality and exploitation of the capitalist-imperialist system, shown how communism would create a fairer, classless society, and be persuaded that revolution was achievable.

Shining Path A Peruvian communist faction that emerged in the late 1960s. Its aim was to overthrow the Peruvian government and establish a communist state. Maoist in nature, Shining Path sought a cultural revolution and the suppression of all elitist and bourgeois elements. In 1980, the movement took up armed struggle, waged guerilla warfare against the Peruvian army and performed numerous political assassinations and bombings, resulting in the death of an estimated 11,000 people. Shining Path is still active, but its membership has fallen in recent years.

state control The running (and as applicable, ownership) of any political, social or business entity by central government. The term is usually, although not exclusively, associated with socialist or communist countries (often with oppressive and authoritarian overtones in the case of the latter).

COMMUNISM

the 30-second politics

Communism encompasses

several diverse schools (for example, Leninism, Maoism and Trotskyism) but all support a commitment to Marxist philosophy, seek to eliminate class distinctions by placing all property under the State's dominion and assist revolutionary movements in other countries seeking to remove capitalist oppression. The basic human conflict is between oppressors and oppressed, and communism seeks to end this domination by empowering workers and creating a classless society. A capitalist society is inherently unjust because workers suffer alienation as they are oppressed by business owners; communists wish to change the social order and apply the principles of science to governance while valuing each member of society equally. Communism is publicly committed to the ideas of Karl Marx and desires to be the only legitimate agent with authority in society. The government takes charge over the economy, society and individual families in an attempt to reshape society so that poverty and oppression are eliminated. Communism requires a working class and needs to emerge from pre-existing capitalist societies.

RELATED THEORIES
See also
MARXISM
page 104
LENINISM
page 108
MAOISM
page 110
SOCIALISM
page 120

3-SECOND SOUNDBITE
Workers rebel to overthrow capitalism and seize ownership of property for the State.

3-MINUTE MANIFESTO
Communism promises to eliminate oppression by removing economic classes, but the historical record demonstrates that alienation increased through the application of communist methods. Communism suffers from a defective understanding of the human person, which is not defined by an economic paradigm. Eliminating economic classes did not remove oppression but created a new form of dominance in which society was subjected to intense state control. The communist attempt to abolish alienation led to unprecedented repression.

3-SECOND BIOGRAPHIES
ANTONIO GRAMSCI
1891–1937
Italian political theorist who identified cultural hegemony as a means of oppression

DAVID HARVEY
1935–
Social theorist and critic of global capitalism

30-SECOND TEXT
G. Doug Davis

'To tell the truth is revolutionary.'
ANTONIO GRAMSCI

MARXISM

the 30-second politics

Marx posited that history itself
was driven by class conflict. Specifically he
believed that any given era of political
development in a specific location was driven
by the relationship between an exploiter class
and the exploited class from which the exploiter
class received its wealth and power. These
classes would eventually come into conflict,
leading to revolutionary change and a new set
of exploiters and exploited who, likewise, would
come into conflict. This process would repeat
itself over time until it eventually resulted in
Utopian communism where there would be
no more classes and human beings could
enjoy the fruits of their own labour without
exploitation. According to Marx, the last stage
of historical development before communism
was capitalism, where the exploiter class
(the capitalist bourgeoisie) owned the capital
(i.e. the means of production) and the exploited
class (the workers, or proletariat) toiled to keep
the capitalists rich until they recognized their
circumstances and overthrew their overlords.
Marxism is a direct intellectual and political
response to the rapidly changing conditions
occurring in Europe during the 19th century
as a result of the Industrial Revolution and the
new and complex social relationships that were
emerging as a result.

3-SECOND SOUNDBITE
Class conflict moves
history ever forward
through revolutionary
conflict until history
itself ends.

3-MINUTE MANIFESTO
Marx thought that work
was fundamental to
human nature and that any
system that did not allow
the worker to control the
results of that work was
exploitation and therefore
utterly unjust. The
foundational idea of
Marx's theories was that
until workers could totally
control the products of
their labour humans could
not fully realize their own
humanity. Under Utopian
communism the excess
product of human labour
would be shared.

RELATED THEORIES
See also
CLASS CONFLICT
page 30
COMMUNISM
page 102
LENINISM
page 108

3-SECOND BIOGRAPHIES
KARL MARX
1818–1883
See pages 106–7

FRIEDRICH ENGELS
1820–1895
Marx's patron and co-author
of *The Communist Manifesto*

VLADIMIR ILYICH
ULYANOV LENIN
1870–1924
Leader of the Russian
Revolution

30-SECOND TEXT
Steven L. Taylor

*'From each according
to his ability, to each
according to his needs!'*
KARL MARX

1818
Born, Trier, Prussia

1835
Attended University of
Bonn before moving to
the University of Berlin

1841
Doctorate from the
University of Jena

1843
Married Jenny von
Westphalen

1848
Published *The Communist
Manifesto*, a joint
collaboration with
Friedrich Engels

1849
Moved to London

1859
Published *A Contribution
to the Critique of the
Political Economy*

1864
Elected to the General
Council of the First
International

1867
Published the first
volume of *Das Kapital*

1871
Published *The Civil War
in France*

1883
Died, London

KARL MARX

Karl Marx was born in Trier,

Prussia, in 1818. He attended university in Berlin, and after completing his doctorate in 1841 Marx became editor of the pro-democracy newspaper *The Rhenish Gazette*. His increasingly left-wing, anti-government stance resulted in strict censorship and he resigned in 1843, moving to Paris to start another newspaper. Paris in the 1840s was the centre of European revolution, and here Marx immersed himself in socialist meetings and the life of the working class. It was in Paris that he formed a firm friendship with Friedrich Engels, with whom he wrote *The Communist Manifesto*. Published on behalf of the Communist League in 1848 – a time of widespread revolutionary unrest in Europe – this short work reviews the history of class struggle and sets out communist plans for the overthrow of the capitalist bourgeoisie and the creation of a classless society.

After being expelled from France and Belgium, Marx finally settled in London in 1849, where, aided by financial support from Engels, he began his exhaustive studies on capitalism, economics, trade and manufacturing. But as well as being a political theorist, Marx was an energetic activist. He was elected to the General Council of the First International in 1864, the aim of which was to unite disparate left-wing groups. In 1867 Marx published the first volume of *Das Kapital*, a dense and often scientific work in which he outlined his concepts of surplus value, the division of labour and the alienation of the working class. Capitalism, he argued in conclusion, would bring about its own downfall.

During the last decade or so of his life, particularly following the savage suppression of the Paris Commune in 1871, Marx became increasingly dejected, and due to failing health was unable to complete the second and third volumes of *Das Kapital* before he died in 1883 in relative obscurity – an almost inconceivable situation when viewed from the perspective of the 21st century.

LENINISM

the 30-second politics

Leninism is a political doctrine
developed by the Russian Bolshevik leader
Vladimir Lenin. It is a variant of Marxism.
According to Marxism, a spontaneous proletarian
uprising would occur only in a country with
full development of industrial capitalism. Lenin
realized that agrarian Russia in the early 20th
century lacked the requisite pre-revolutionary
conditions. To develop a pragmatic theoretical
base for socialist transition at the time, he
adapted Marxism to the circumstances of
Russia, turning Marxism from a Utopian theory
to revolutionary reality. Lenin suggested that
during the period of imperialism, underdeveloped
countries such as Russia might feature the first
proletariat revolution instead of advanced
industrial countries because the latter, in order
to avoid revolution, could strengthen capitalism
and smooth domestic labour-capital relations
using profits from colony exploitation. Lenin
believed that the working class would develop
revolutionary consciousness and overthrow
capitalism only under the guide of a vanguard
of professional revolutionaries, who were drawn
mainly from the bourgeois intelligentsia. He
emphasized the exclusive leadership of the
Communist Party in assuming power and
establishing a government of 'proletariat
dictatorship' until the State withers away.

RELATED THEORIES
See also
COMMUNISM
page 102
MARXISM
page 104
MAOISM
page 110

3-SECOND BIOGRAPHY
VLADIMIR I. LENIN
1870–1924
Russian revolutionary and leader
of the Soviet state (1917–1924)

30-SECOND TEXT
Feng Sun

3-SECOND SOUNDBITE
Leninism proposes a short
cut to Marxist utopia –
socialist revolution and
proletarian dictatorship.

3-MINUTE MANIFESTO
Leninism grew out of
Marxism. However,
whether Leninism
represents a contribution
to or a corruption of
Marxism has been
debated. The opponents
argue that Leninism
reversed the order of
economics over politics
by denying the necessity
of a fully developed
capitalism right before
the spontaneous
proletariat revolution.
As a concrete guideline
for proletariat revolution,
Leninism was to
fundamentally influence
the development of
communism in the Soviet
Union and elsewhere for
seven decades.

*'A revolutionary class
cannot but wish for
the defeat of its
government in a
reactionary war.'*
VLADIMIR LENIN

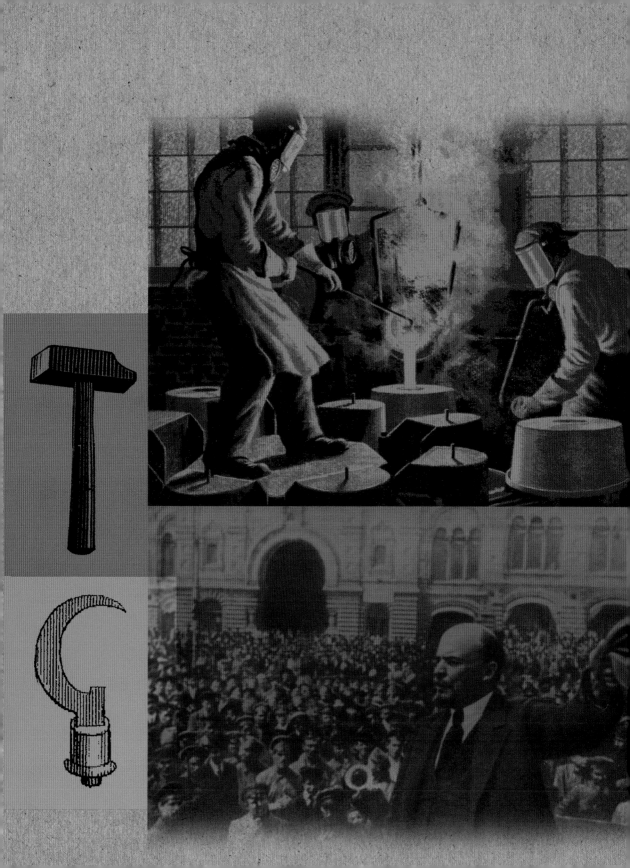

MAOISM

the 30-second politics

Maosim is the term used to describe the specific variation of revolutionary communism developed by Mao Zedong in China. In its most generic usage it refers to revolutionary change via mobilization of the peasantry as opposed to the urban proletariat. Like Lenin, Mao took the basic tenets of Marx's theory of class conflict and adapted them to the reality around him. While the basics of Marx's view of the progress of history dictated that communist revolution could only take place in the context of advanced capitalism, Mao believed that the theory could be adapted to the peasant-based society of China of the 1930s and 1940s. Mao himself described his approach as 'Marxism adapted for Chinese circumstances'. Mao was the son of a relatively prosperous pig farmer, and worked the fields as a child, and so had a direct understanding of the peasant life. A central tenet of Maoism was permanent revolution, including violence as a tool: progress required turmoil and therefore the revolution was never entirely over. Mao vehemently opposed elitism, even within the Chinese Communist Party. Although Maoism died with him in China, it remained a theory of choice for revolutionary groups elsewhere, including the Khmer Rouge in Cambodia and the Shining Path in Peru.

RELATED THEORIES
See also
COMMUNISM
page 102
MARXISM
page 104
LENINISM
page 108

3-SECOND BIOGRAPHIES
MAO ZEDONG
1893–1976
First president of the People's Republic of China

DENG XIAOPING
1904–1997
Secretary General of the Chinese Communist Party

30-SECOND TEXT
Steven L. Taylor

3-SECOND SOUNDBITE
Peasants rise up to revolt against their feudal overlords to create a communist state.

3-MINUTE MANIFESTO
Mao had been one of the founding members of the Chinese Communist Party when it was established by the Moscow-based Comintern in 1921. By 1949, he had proclaimed himself president of the newly formed People's Republic of China. Free from Russian intervention, he used fear, manipulation, propaganda and death squads to forge the country in his own image: anti-intellectual, anti-elite, anti-tradition. He oversaw the Great Leap Forward (destruction of traditional farming methods) and the Cultural Revolution (destruction of intellectualism).

'The guerrilla must move among the people as a fish swims in the sea.'
MAO ZEDONG

ANARCHO-SYNDICALISM

the 30-second politics

Governments are inherently
unjust because they protect private property
and maintain the dominance of the rich over
the poor. No state authority is adequate to
protect or improve worker needs and the
only solution is to eliminate government.
Anarcho-syndicalism proposes a revolution
where workers take control of businesses and
industries and destroy all authority outside trade
unions. The new social order will not have a
government or even a large trade union, but
be composed of separate worker groups that
manage and control each business separately.
The resulting unions will be structured to give
each worker an equal voice and vote in deciding
the organization's action. Anarcho-syndicalism
attempts to eliminate social classes, capitalism,
private property and all forms of social
authority, including religious faith, to empower
individual workers. Communism does not
provide a sufficient model to free labour
because it proposes a central authority that acts
on its behalf. Anarcho-syndicalism attempts to
eliminate economic classes while empowering
labourers to make their own decisions with no
outside influence or control.

3-SECOND SOUNDBITE
Anarcho-syndicalism
proposes popular revolution
to eliminate the State and
empower trade unions.

3-MINUTE MANIFESTO
Anarcho-syndicalism
provides a strong critique
of communism by showing
that workers will continue
to be oppressed through
the centralized political
power. The correction to
this error creates problems
because the relations
between trade unions
will not automatically
be harmonious. The
elimination of the central
political authority also
removes the means to
settle disputes that would
emerge between unions
and therefore the goal
of social unity will not
be achieved.

RELATED THEORIES
See also
LIBERTARIANISM
page 72
MARXISM
page 104
SOCIALISM
page 120

3-SECOND BIOGRAPHIES
PIERRE-JOSEPH PROUDHON
1809-1865
French anarchist who wrote that
property is theft

NOAM CHOMSKY
1928–
Linguist, political activist
and proponent of
anarcho-syndicalism

30-SECOND TEXT
G. Doug Davis

*'Unfortunately, you
can't vote the rascals
out, because you never
voted them in, in the
first place.'*
NOAM CHOMSKY

POLITICAL ECONOMY

POLITICAL ECONOMY
GLOSSARY

deregulation In economics, the process of removing government restrictions and regulations with a view to creating a freer market.

fair trade A socioeconomic movement that aims to improve the working and trading conditions of those workers and farmers in developing countries who are involved in the production or manufacture of goods that are exported to developed countries.

fiscal policy In economics, the method by which government can moderate the economy through spending and taxation.

free market A market economy in which there is no government interference in the form of regulation or subsidy. In a free market price is governed purely by the theory of supply and demand.

invisible hand In economics, term first used by Adam Smith to describe how a free market regulates itself through competition, the supply and demand equilibrium, and the fact that all participants aim to maximize self-interest. The concept has been described as an economic version of Darwin's theory of natural selection.

laissez faire (French 'leave to do') An economic term used to describe a market that is free from government intervention. The phrase dates back to the late 17th century, but was picked up and popularized by classical economists in the mid 19th century.

macroeconomy The economy of a large socioeconomic entity such as a state or region, a country, group of countries or even the global economy. Macroeconomics is concerned with large-scale, aggregated economic phenomena such as national income, rate of growth, inflation and gross domestic product (GDP). The macroeconomy contrasts with the microeconomy, which refers to the economy at the level of companies and individuals.

market socialist economy Any economic system in which capital and the means of production are owned cooperatively or by the State, but one in which market forces, based on supply and demand and a free price system, determine production.

monetarism Economic theory that holds that the amount of money in circulation in an economy determines key economic indicators such as national output, inflation and price stability.

nationalization The bringing into national ownership of any privately owned businesses, corporations or resources. Nationalization is mainly associated with socialist or communist governments and is viewed by its proponents as a means of creating social and economic equality. The post-Second World War British Labour government nationalized a number of key industries including rail, steel and coal.

privatization The sale of state-owned businesses, corporations or resources to the private sector. Governments, whether local or national, tend to privatize either to raise revenue, cut costs or to create more cost-efficient services due to free-market competition. During the 1980s governments of both the United States and the United Kingdom privatized large swathes of nationally owned assets as part of fiscal conservatism's deregulatory ideology.

protectionism Government policy that restricts international trade through the introduction of tariffs, subsidies or import quotas. Protectionist actions seek to protect domestic industries (and workers) from foreign competition. Opponents of protectionism argue that over time the policy stifles domestic growth, leading to a reduction in output and economic welfare.

recession In economics, a period of economic decline. More specifically a country is said to be in recession if there is a reduction in gross domestic product (GDP) for two consecutive quarters. Indicators associated with recession include increased unemployment and a fall in stock exchanges and housing markets.

stagflation A contraction of 'stagnation' and 'inflation'. In economics, a condition of slow growth coupled with high inflation and unemployment. Once considered an almost impossible situation (as high unemployment usually accompanies low inflation and vice versa), the oil crisis of the 1970s caused prices to rise sharply while also slowing the economy.

supply and demand A fundamental economic principle that determines price. Essentially the price of a good is determined when the point at which the quantity supplied equals the quantity demanded.

tariff A protectionist measure in which government imposes a tax on imported goods. The idea behind tariffs is to protect domestic goods (and therefore the workforce) from potentially cheaper foreign imports.

CAPITALISM

the 30-second politics

If you live in a capitalist economy, every time you go to the beauty salon to have your hair styled, or when you go to the shop to purchase a packet of sweets, or even if you stuff your money under the mattress of your bed, you are helping determine the prices of goods, the unemployment rate and how much interest banks charge their customers. Capitalist nations rely upon the free decisions of self-interested private groups – which includes both private citizens like you and me as well as enormous corporations – to allocate a nation's resources. Capitalism is both an ideal as well as a set of real-life institutions and practices that fall considerably short of that ideal. Many nations today, including most nations in Europe and North America, are capitalist because the means of economic production and exchange in these nations are privately owned and operated. Though economists speak of free markets, every nation in the world has opted for significant government intervention into their economies through taxation, welfare spending and economic regulations (among other methods). Where to draw the line between a capitalist economy and a mixed economy, or even a socialist economy, is far from settled.

RELATED THEORIES
See also
CLASSICAL LIBERALISM
page 64
LIBERTARIANISM
page 72
KEYNESIANISM
page 124
MERCANTILISM
page 126

3-SECOND BIOGRAPHIES
ADAM SMITH
1723–1790
Scottish free-market economist

FRIEDRICH HAYEK
1899–1992
Austrian capitalist economist

MILTON FRIEDMAN
1912–2006
US economist and proponent of free-market ideas

30-SECOND TEXT
Michael E. Bailey

3-SECOND SOUNDBITE
In a capitalist economic system private groups holding private property freely exchange private goods and services for private profit.

3-MINUTE MANIFESTO
Capitalism depends upon capital, and capital is the economists' fancy term for savings. Savings, in turn, requires that one does *not* succumb to the new digital camera in the shop window calling out your name. Capitalism, in other words, depends upon self-discipline and delayed gratification. At the same time, capitalist economies daily bombard consumers to indulge all of their hedonistic consumer fantasies. Noting this contradiction, some social thinkers have speculated that capitalism contains the seeds of its own demise.

'History suggests that capitalism is a necessary condition for political freedom.'
MILTON FRIEDMAN

SOCIALISM

the 30-second politics

Socialism, generally defined, is a political and economic theory that advocates popular control of either the whole economy or major sectors of it. Various strains of socialist thought have emerged throughout history; some early socialist thinkers, such as Henri de Saint-Simon and Robert Owen, promoted a 'Utopian socialist' ideal in which self-sufficient colonies would break away from existing economies and tend to their own needs in isolation from the rest of the world. Later socialists advocated revolutionary change in society to impose a socialist order, most notably communist thinkers such as Karl Marx, Friedrich Engels and Vladimir Lenin; others, such as Eduard Bernstein, argued for either a gradual transition to socialism through democratic means, or the development of a 'mixed' or market socialist model in which some, but not all, aspects of the economy would be subject to popular control. This approach became dominant in Western Europe after the Second World War, with countries implementing some degree of nationalization of industry and central planning, without rejecting the entire capitalist system; this 'postwar' consensus lasted into the 1970s. China, since the death of Mao Zedong, has gradually introduced a 'market socialist' economic system, albeit with heavy state involvement in the direction of investment.

3-SECOND SOUNDBITE
Socialism is an economic theory favouring total or partial public control of the economy.

3-MINUTE MANIFESTO
The ideals of socialism remain appealing to many, despite their mixed record in practice over the past century. The Venezuelan government under Hugo Chávez has promoted a 'Bolivarian Alternative' economic strategy that rejects capitalism in favour of a socialist economic programme and barter-based international trade; however, long-term viability depends on the continued economic value of Venezuela's petroleum exports to capitalist countries such as the United States. Chávez's views, however, have found favour with other left-wing and centre-left Latin American leaders.

RELATED THEORIES
See also
SOCIAL DEMOCRACY
page 74
MARXISM
page 104
KEYNESIANISM
page 124

3-SECOND BIOGRAPHIES
HENRI DE SAINT-SIMON
1760–1825
French aristocrat whose Utopian socialist ideas inspired later thinkers

CLEMENT ATTLEE
1883–1967
British prime minister who implemented a market socialist programme

30-SECOND TEXT
Christopher N. Lawrence

'The inherent vice of capitalism is the unequal sharing of blessings; the inherent virtue of socialism is the equal sharing of miseries.'
WINSTON CHURCHILL

GLOBALIZATION

the 30-second politics

Globalization is the name given to the trend, arguably ongoing since the latter part of the 19th century, toward a greater integration of national and regional economies into a larger, unified global economic system based on freer trade in goods, services and investment capital. Globalization's early stages can be traced back to the middle part of the 19th century, when Britain – then the world's leading economic and military power – began to change its economic policies away from protectionism and mercantilism toward lowering tariffs on goods traded with countries outside the British Empire and broader sphere of influence. The two World Wars and the Great Depression led to a reduction in international trade, but after the Second World War, as the United States replaced Britain as the leading developed economy it adopted a similar outlook toward free trade, at least in areas where free trade benefited American business interests. Today globalization is not simply a matter of trade in raw materials and manufactured goods. It also encompasses trade in services and investment opportunities, which leads to an even more tightly integrated economy in which many key agents in major economic sectors of most developed and developing economies are controlled by either foreign-owned or transnational corporations.

3-SECOND SOUNDBITE
Globalization is the increasing degree of interconnection between national economies.

3-MINUTE MANIFESTO
Economic integration has faced strong criticism in many countries as formerly protected economic sectors have been exposed to international competition. Some critics have rejected the idea of globalization entirely, while others seek greater regulation of economic integration, such as the promotion of 'fair trade' (incorporating greater protection for both workers and the environment in the developing world) rather than free trade, and describe themselves as pro 'alter-globalization' rather than opponents of globalization per se.

RELATED THEORIES
See also
CAPITALISM
page 118
MERCANTILISM
page 126
NEOLIBERALISM
page 128

3-SECOND BIOGRAPHIES
JOSÉ BOVÉ
1953–
French agriculture unionist and a leading figure in both the 'anti-globalization' and 'alter-globalization' movements

THOMAS FRIEDMAN
1953–
Columnist, author and proponent of globalization

30-SECOND TEXT
Christopher N. Lawrence

'People have accused me of being in favour of globalization. This is equivalent to accusing me of being in favour of the sun rising in the morning.'
CLARE SHORT

KEYNESIANISM

the 30-second politics

Keynesianism refers to a theory of macroeconomics named after the English economist John Maynard Keynes. It is an opposite of laissez faire economic thought, advocating a role for government in the economy. According to Keynesianism, the cyclical economic downturn is due to insufficient aggregate demand. Contrary to the conventional wisdom, Keynesianism suggests that the capitalist market economy does not have a mechanism to address the problem quickly. In such a case, active policy response by the government is the most effective solution, especially fiscal policy actions to expand public spending and cut tax. The rationale is that by deficit spending on new public projects or cutting taxes, government creates more jobs and injects income, which results in more spending in the general economy, stimulating economic activities and reducing unemployment. Government intervention then restores the virtuous circle between demand and supply, driving an underperforming economy back on track. Politically, Keynesianism advocates a large government sector as a necessary lever to stabilize the economy. In the period from the Second World War through the early 1970s, Keynesianism had greatest influence in Western industrialized countries. Its credibility declined when stagflation hit the global capital system in the 1970s.

RELATED THEORIES
See also
CAPITALISM
page 118
SOCIALISM
page 120

3-SECOND SOUNDBITE
Keynesianism advocates the manipulation of fiscal policies to manage the economy.

3-MINUTE MANIFESTO
Keynesianism believes that economic recessions could be cured by government corrective interventions. This belief is based on the assumption that government is knowledgeable and capable enough to make valuable judgments in arranging an economy. Keynesian policy was attacked by monetarists for being misconceived government fiscal actions that would lead to high inflation and crowd out private investment. Despite all the criticism, Keynesian economic reasoning has continued to serve as the basis of much contemporary economic policy.

3-SECOND BIOGRAPHY
JOHN MAYNARD KEYNES
1883–1946
Father of macroeconomics and arguably the most influential economist of the 20th century

30-SECOND TEXT
Feng Sun

'It is better to be roughly right than precisely wrong.'
JOHN MAYNARD KEYNES

MERCANTILISM

the 30-second politics

Mercantilism refers to the economic thought and practice prevailing in Europe throughout the 16th–18th centuries, which emphasized a protectionist role for the government in building a powerful state. A state's power was dependent on its national wealth, which was defined in terms of gold and silver reserves. Since the amount of world wealth was 'unchangeable', a state could only increase its wealth and power at the expense of other states. Based on these perceptions, mercantilist states exercised strict policies to ensure a positive balance of trade by restraining imports and encouraging exports through tariffs and subsidies. Domestic production was largely encouraged and carefully regulated by the government to maintain economic self-sufficiency as well as an advantage in foreign markets. A merchant marine and naval fleet was built to secure exclusive trade privilege and to conquer overseas colonies that served as supplies of raw materials to the mother country and markets for finished products. In history, the mercantilist era was associated with the aggressive trading activities by merchants such as the British East India Company, the ruthless exploitations of colonies in America, Asia and Africa and the military competitions among major sea powers.

3-SECOND SOUNDBITE
Mercantilism is economic nationalism under the law of the jungle.

3-MINUTE MANIFESTO
The term 'mercantilism' was first used by Adam Smith to criticize a system directly opposed to free trade and laissez faire. Mercantilism emphasized state protectionism and governmental regulations, which largely limited economic freedom and vitality. The 'beggar thy neighbour' policy fuelled a continuous cycle of intra-European conflicts since it was impossible for all states to have a trade surplus. However, mercantilism did play an important role in state building and economic unification in early modern Europe.

RELATED THEORIES
See also
REALISM
page 138
IMPERIALISM
page 142

3-SECOND BIOGRAPHIES
THOMAS MUN
1571–1641
English economist and writer; the last of the early mercantilists

ADAM SMITH
1723–1790
English economist and opponent of mercantilism

30-SECOND TEXT
Feng Sun

'We must always take heed that we buy no more from strangers than we sell them; for so should we impoverish ourselves and enrich them.'
SIR THOMAS SMITH

NEOLIBERALISM

the 30-second politics

Neoliberalism refers to a set of economic policy prescriptions emphasizing the primacy of the market over the government. The 'neo' indicates that it is an updated version of classical realism, dating back to the political theorist Adam Smith in the 18th century. His book *The Wealth of Nations* famously argued that an 'invisible hand' of the market ensured that seeking private gain would lead to the common good. Neoliberalism asserts that both economic growth and prosperity are best achieved by drastically cutting government spending, privatizing state-owned industries, deregulating, expanding trade and encouraging foreign investment. Following basic laws of supply and demand, a free market will ensure that resources are allocated efficiently, which benefits everyone. These policies are placed in counterpoint to statist models of development, which are viewed as contributing to economic stagnation and debt in the developing world during the decades after the Second World War. Advocates point to countries in the developing world that had adopted neoliberal policies and thereby tamed inflation, generated economic growth and reduced poverty. Such policies have been central to the growth of economic globalization.

RELATED THEORIES
See also
CLASSICAL LIBERALISM
page 64
LIBERTARIANISM
page 72
CAPITALISM
page 118
OBJECTIVISM
page 132

3-SECOND BIOGRAPHIES
ADAM SMITH
1729–1790
Scottish political theorist who advocated a free market

MILTON FRIEDMAN
1912–2006
Influential US economist; he opposed government intervention and supported a return to free-market economics

30-SECOND TEXT
Gregory Weeks

'It is not from the benevolence of the butcher, the brewer, or the baker that we expect our dinner, but from their regard to their own interest.'
ADAM SMITH

3-SECOND SOUNDBITE
For neoliberals, everyone's visible economic decisions turn into an invisible hand, while government keeps hands off.

3-MINUTE MANIFESTO
Since the 1980s in particular, neoliberal policies have been very controversial, especially in the developing world. The combination of privatization and subsidy reductions sparked riots in numerous countries and in several cases even led to the overthrow of presidents. Protests and the election of more statist-oriented presidents are marked by explicit rejection of neoliberal models.

1905
Born, St Petersburg,
Russia

1922
Attended the University
of Petrograd

1925
Moved to the United
States

1929
Married actor Frank
O'Connor

1936
Published a semi-
autobiographical novel
We the Living

1943
Published *The
Fountainhead*

1951
Left Los Angeles for New
York

1957
Published *Atlas Shrugged*

1962
Founded *The Objectivist
Newsletter*

1974
Diagnosed with lung
cancer

1982
Died, New York City

AYN RAND

It's unsurprising that someone with views as controversial as Ayn Rand would have such a polarizing effect – you either love her or hate her.

Born in 1905 in St Petersburg, Russia, Rand was from a wealthy family. Growing up she experienced the social and political upheaval of the Russian Revolution, yet it was thanks to the Bolsheviks that as a Jewish woman she was able to attend university in Petrograd (St Petersburg). However her experiences under communism were to have a profound effect.

In 1925 Rand was allowed to visit relatives in the United States, and she soon moved to Los Angeles to become a writer. Although she achieved some literary success during the 1930s, it was her novel *The Fountainhead* (1943) that brought her to the public's attention. Rand's novel, featuring a young, principled architect's struggle against convention and nepotism, was a precursor to her philosophical works. During the 1950s Rand became increasingly active in politics – and while her vehement anti-communist/pro-individualist free-market stance attracted right-wing supporters, her equally vehement atheism was less well-received.

In 1957 Rand published her most celebrated novel, *Atlas Shrugged*. A bestselling work of fiction, the book is a vehicle for Rand's objectivist philosophy (outlined in a 70-page speech given by John Galt, a character in the novel). Objectivism draws on the Aristotelian tradition of empirical reasoning, self-realization and ethical egoism – which as a political theory translates into anti-statism, libertarianism and laissez faire capitalism.

Often criticized, often lauded, but always outspoken, Rand spent the 1960s and 1970s promoting objectivism through lectures, interviews and her periodical *The Objectivist Newsletter*, to which Alan Greenspan was a notable contributor. Interest in objectivism as a political movement waned following Rand's death in 1982, but the recent global recession and ensuing distrust of government has seen a revival – John Galt is alive and well.

OBJECTIVISM

the 30-second politics

Objectivism is Ayn Rand's

philosophy that links objective reality, reason, self-interest and capitalism to form a system that proposes a template for society where individuals can act for their own happiness and protect their long-term survival. People may desire what they wish, but to achieve their goals they must first have a correct understanding of reality. This allows individuals to use reason to advance their self-interest in a world where capitalism and limited government provide the capacity for personal action. The State is reduced to protecting individual rights, preventing violence and providing free-market exchanges that allow people to engage in advantageous trade. A government should not propose values or provide essentials to needy persons, but only work to preserve individual rights. Objectivism rejects traditional Western ethics and provides an early defence for the sexual revolution and legalized abortion; it provides equal rights to women but rejects modern feminism. Objectivism offers an original defence of individual rights and laissez faire capitalism that rejects the traditional arguments proposed by John Locke or Adam Smith.

RELATED THEORIES
See also
LIBERTARIANISM
page 72
CAPITALISM
page 118

3-SECOND BIOGRAPHIES
ALAN GREENSPAN
1926–
Former Federal Reserve chairman and Rand supporter

NATHANIEL BRANDEN
(Born BLUMENTHAL)
1930–
Psychologist and objectivist lecturer

30-SECOND TEXT
G. Doug Davis

3-SECOND SOUNDBITE
Objectivism is a philosophy that when applied to politics advocated capitalism and limited government to enable individuals to pursue self-interest.

3-MINUTE MANIFESTO
Rand's works generated a passionate following, but were never accepted by academics or wider American culture. Her protagonist is the rational individual who is independent and who acts alone to secure happiness. Rand's weakness is that this hero, following her prescribed path, will find neither security nor freedom. The model Rand offers has no satisfactory end because it leads to endless repetition of the prescribed method.

'I never found beauty in longing for the impossible and never found the possible to be beyond my reach.'
AYN RAND

INTERNATIONAL RELATIONS

cultural hegemony The cultural dominance of one group, state or nation over others. The Italian Marxist theorist Antonio Gramsci used the term to describe the dominance of one class over another, to the point at which the subordinate class accepts the world order of the dominant class as 'natural'. Today the term is used more to describe the domination of popular culture (in the form of television programmes, movies, brands, etc.) from one nation over others.

decolonization The process during which former colonies achieve independence from the colonial power. Periods of decolonization have occurred throughout history, with the last great period taking place soon after the Second World War, when formerly powerful European countries, such as Britain and France, could no longer afford to maintain control over their former colonies and were encouraged to decolonize by the emerging powers of the United States and the Soviet Union.

Kyoto Protocol An international treaty under which 37 industrialized nations have agreed to an overall reduction of the main greenhouse gases – carbon dioxide, nitrous oxide, methane, sulphur hexafluoride, HFCs and PFCs. The agreement was adopted in 1997 and came into force in 2005. Reduction targets range from 7 per cent for the United States, 8 per cent for Europe and 6 per cent for Japan to 0 per cent for Russia with, additionally, allowable increases for Australia and Iceland.

mutual destruction (fully mutual assured destruction – MAD) A military term that first came into use during the Cold War when nuclear armament was at an all-time high. Essentially it described the scenario in which both the United States (and its allies) and the Soviet Union (and its allies) would be entirely destroyed by nuclear weapons following a pre-emptive nuclear strike by either side. Proponents of MAD as a military strategy argue that it is the ultimate nuclear deterrent.

pre-emptive war Any war that is undertaken in order to prevent a perceived attack or threat. Considered by proponents as a form of self-defence, two recent examples of pre-emptive wars have been the US-led coalition invasion of Iraq and the war in Afghanistan, both of which were prosecuted to prevent terrorist attack. However, in the case of the former there exists doubt over the scale and reality of the perceived threat, while in the latter critics have argued that diplomatic options were not fully explored.

protectionism Government policy that restricts international trade through the introduction of tariffs, subsidies or import quotas. Protectionist actions seek to protect domestic industries (and workers) from foreign competition. Opponents of protectionism argue that over time the policy stifles domestic growth, leading to a reduction in output and economic welfare.

secessionist movement Any group whose purpose is to withdraw membership of a federation or political body, usually in order to secure political independence from the usually larger, more powerful political entity. The term is synonymous with separatist movement.

sectarian A term used to describe affiliation or association with a religious denomination or sect. Sectarian violence, for example, describes unrest between two opposing religious factions.

REALISM

the 30-second politics

Realism is an international
relations theory that focuses on power and
national self-interest. Although there are
many variations of the theory, they all rest
on the idea that since there is no world
government that can serve as law-enforcer,
states will act rationally to protect themselves.
This anarchic system means states use whatever
power they have to stay secure. Military force
is the ultimate weapon for states, and realism
expects conflict to occur as states try to
advance themselves in relation to their
counterparts. Other elements of national power
include economic capabilities, abundance of
raw materials, political stability or even cultural
hegemony. At the same time, though, realism
explains the absence of war. During the Cold
War, the United States and the Soviet Union
never fought each other directly. Each country
knew the other had nuclear weapons and that
a war would result in mutual destruction, thus
damaging their own security. In fact, some
prominent realists, such as Kenneth Waltz,
argue that the spread of nuclear weapons to
more countries would not necessarily be a bad
thing, because if all countries have them, none
will use them.

3-SECOND SOUNDBITE
In the international
system, the most powerful
make the rules and rule
the powerless.

3-MINUTE MANIFESTO
Realists think individual
leaders and international
institutions are not
important, arguing that
we can understand how
states interact by looking
at the array of their
capabilities and their
place in the international
system. Critics, though,
point to significant
differences that leaders
(for example, Winston
Churchill versus Neville
Chamberlain or Jimmy
Carter versus Ronald
Reagan) may have on
relations with other
countries, and to the
fact that international
institutions can play
an influential role in
international politics.

RELATED THEORIES
See also
NEOCONSERVATISM
page 144
CONSTRUCTIVISM
page 150

3-SECOND BIOGRAPHIES
HANS MORGENTHAU
1904–1980
See pages 140–1

HENRY KISSINGER
1923–
Political scientist and former US
Secretary of State

KENNETH WALTZ
1924–
Leading figure in international
relations theory

30-SECOND TEXT
Gregory Weeks

'Man is born to seek
power, yet his actual
condition makes him
a slave to the power
of others.'
HANS MORGENTHAU

1904
Born Coburg, Germany

1932
Taught law at the
University of Geneva

1935
Moved to teach law at
the University of Madrid

1937
Emigrated to the United
States; teaches at
Brooklyn College

1939
Taught at University of
Kansas City

1943
Accepted teaching
position at the University
of Chicago

1946
Published *Scientific Man
Vs. Power Politics*

1948
Published *Politics among
Nations*

1951
Published *In Defense of
the National Interest*

1960
Published *The Purpose of
American Politics*

1979
Dies, New York City

HANS MORGENTHAU

One of the 20th century's

foremost political thinkers, specifically in the sphere of international politics, Hans Morgenthau will be best remembered for his realist theories of politics.

Born in Germany in 1904, the son of a Jewish doctor, Morgenthau grew up in a postwar Germany in economic and military ruin. In the early 1920s he attended university in Frankfurt and Munich, initially studying philosophy before switching to law. After graduating he continued his studies in Geneva and following teaching posts in Geneva and Madrid he emigrated to the United States in 1937. Morgenthau settled at the University of Chicago in 1942, where he taught until 1971.

In his first major work, *Scientific Man Vs. Power Politics* (1946), Morgenthau was critical of the prevalent contemporary belief that science was the answer to the world's social and political problems. In his second book, *Politics among Nations* (1948), he outlined the concept of political realism.

Primarily concerned with international relations, this book argued that international politics was shaped by the national interests of sovereign states and was therefore essentially about states 'keeping power, increasing power and demonstrating power'. As a realist, Morgenthau believed that the policies of nation states should be removed from the universal morals that are experienced by individuals. States should seek to increase their power over any other moral or legal considerations.

Morgenthau's work was hugely influential, and during the Cold War period he was a policy consultant to the US State Department. However, he was also critical of US foreign policy – opposing the war in Vietnam, for example – and although primarily thought of as a power-politics realist, often overlooked are his endeavours to tease out the connection between moral principles and the politics of necessity, a theme explored in his work *In Defense of the National Interest* (1951).

IMPERIALISM

the 30-second politics

Imperialism is based on a

dominant relationship that a country has over another, with one being far more powerful than the other and using that power to exploit the resources of the weaker to its advantage. The most literal version involves seizing territories, such as in a colonial system, where the stronger takes over the political and economic reins entirely. Examples include the British, Chinese, Spanish and Portuguese empires, which sprawled over wide areas. That in turn led to mercantilism, whereby the colonizer insisted on exclusive trade with the colonies, which generated considerable resentment. The term took on an even broader meaning with the rise of Marxism-Leninism, which viewed all advanced capitalist countries as part of an economic imperialist project that kept less-developed countries in poverty despite not ruling directly. Thus, the state of being hegemonic – far more powerful than others – qualified as imperialism. Either way, the government of a strong state directs the political and economic machinery of others, sometimes even over very long distances. This can also lead to cultural imperialism, where the culture of the more powerful state becomes dominant over its local counterpart.

3-SECOND SOUNDBITE
Empires spread their influence far and wide, enveloping weaker countries and using their resources in a way that makes them weaker still.

3-MINUTE MANIFESTO
In the past, imperialism was openly applauded, particularly in Europe, and justified for its supposed civilizing influence over more 'backward' peoples. Particularly after the wave of decolonization of the post-World War era, however, the term has taken on clearly negative connotations and has become an insult.

RELATED THEORIES
See also
MARXISM
page 104
LENINISM
page 108
MERCANTILISM
page 126

3-SECOND BIOGRAPHIES
VLADIMIR I. LENIN
1870–1924
Communist leader who argued that imperialism was the final stage of capitalism

WILLIAM APPLEMAN WILLIAMS
1921–1990
Theorist and critic of American foreign policy

30-SECOND TEXT
Gregory Weeks

'If it were necessary to give the briefest possible definition of imperialism, we should have to say that imperialism is the monopoly stage of capitalism.'
VLADIMIR LENIN

NEOCONSERVATISM

the 30-second politics

Neoconservatism is a term that has been used with some frequency in the public discourse over the last 10 years because of its association with the foreign policy of President George W. Bush and especially the war in Iraq. The origin of the term was as a label to describe disillusioned liberals (in the American political sense of the word) of the early 1970s who believed in a role for government but were critical of the development of the US welfare state and who saw the Democratic Party and American liberals as being insufficient in their anti-communism. Chief among this group was commentator Irving Kristol, often described as the 'godfather of neoconservatism', as well as Norman Podhoretz and Jeanne Kirkpatrick. The views of neoconservatives could be read specifically in the opinion journals *Commentary*, *The Public Interest* and *The National Interest*. William Kristol (son of Irving), founder and editor of the *Weekly Standard* and a regular analyst on the Fox News Channel, has continued the tradition of neoconservative commentary. The younger Kristol is also a co-founder of the Project for the New American Century (PNAC), a think-tank dedicated to a neoconservative vision of US foreign policy which promotes the notion of American hegemony as a positive force in global affairs.

3-SECOND SOUNDBITE
Neoconservatives believe power in the international system can be used as a tool of good by spreading democracy and maintaining US hegemony.

3-MINUTE MANIFESTO
Neoconservatism, as an approach in international relations, is a critique of realism. Instead of seeing the international system as one populated by amoral, rational states that each have their own unique self-interests, neoconservatism sees those states as being either good or evil. As such, the exercise of power against evil states to further the morals of the good states is justifiable. This approach helped fuel the intellectual underpinnings of the Bush doctrine of pre-emptive war.

RELATED THEORIES
See also
CONSERVATISM
page 68
NEOLIBERALISM
page 128
REALISM
page 138

3-SECOND BIOGRAPHIES
LEO STRAUSS
1899–1973
Political philosopher and intellectual source of neoconservatism
IRVING KRISTOL
1920–2009
Author, publisher and 'godfather of neoconservatism'

30-SECOND TEXT
Steven L. Taylor

'A neoconservative is a liberal who has been mugged by reality.'
IRVING KRISTOL

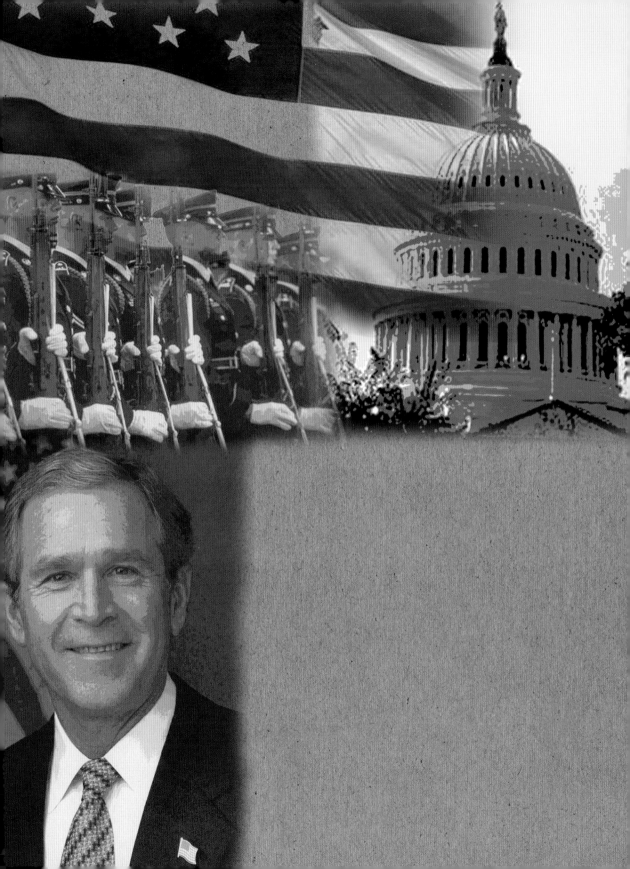

NATIONALISM

the 30-second politics

Nationalism is a deeply felt

common identification among a group of people, with a firm commitment to the advancement of those who are part of that group. This connection can be based on many different factors, such as race, ethnicity, language, religion and/or cultural practices. The concept developed after the French Revolution of 1789, which was the dawning of a new era in which individuals felt part of a broader nation rather than simply beholden to a local ruler. This does not mean that local identification disappears, but rather that the nation claims more allegiance than any other source of authority. Nationalism often does not correspond precisely to the boundaries of states, because people may identify more with someone from another country. For example, Iraqi Kurds feel more Kurdish (as with Kurds in Turkey) than Iraqi. In other cases, as with the Palestinian people, nationalism exists even without a state. Nationalism becomes embedded in many parts of daily life, including education, literature, music and flags. Control over the State – or creation of new states – is obviously a primary goal of nationalists because that is the avenue through which resources can best be obtained to achieve nationalist aims.

3-SECOND SOUNDBITE
Nationalism involves a high level of identification with other people, but also involves a high level of difference with those outside the group.

3-MINUTE MANIFESTO
Nationalism is often the cause of armed conflict, even within a single country. Spain, for example, has three main nations within it, which has led to secessionist movements and violence. In recent years, the same has been true on an even larger scale in Afghanistan and Iraq, where nationalism in the form of sectarian violence, as well as fighting between certain factions and US-led coalition forces, has resulted in the loss of thousands of lives.

RELATED THEORIES
See also
POPULAR SOVEREIGNTY
page 26
FASCISM
page 38
REALISM
page 138

3-SECOND BIOGRAPHIES
SUN YAT-SEN
1866–1925
Chinese nationalist leader

MUSTAFA KEMAL ATATÜRK
1881–1938
First president of Turkey who used the power of nationalism to forge modern Turkey

ERNEST GELLNER
1925–1995
Scholar who wrote on the subject of nationalism

30-SECOND TEXT
Gregory Weeks

'Patriotism is nationalism, and always leads to war.'
HELEN CALDICOTT

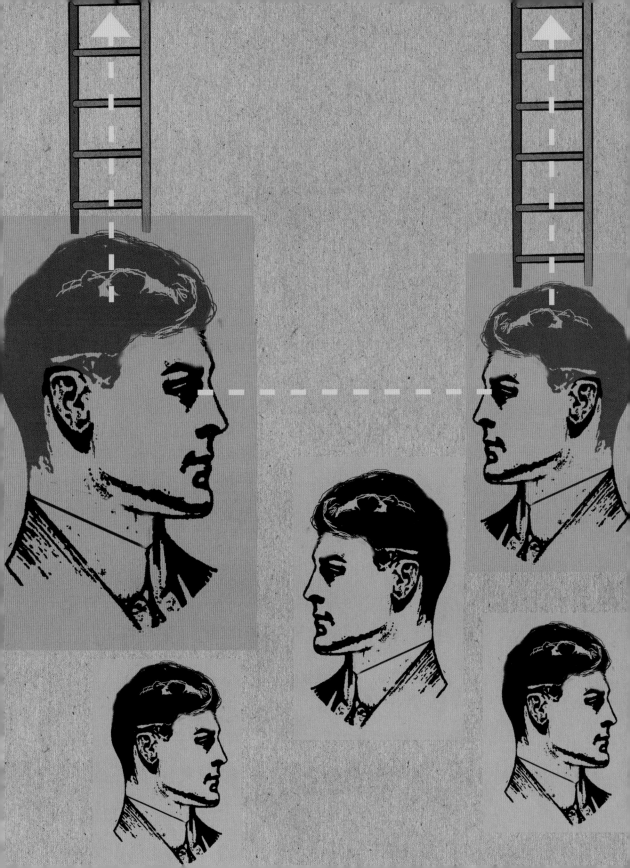

ENVIRONMENTALISM

the 30-second politics

Environmentalism encompasses
a varied set of beliefs that examines the
relationship between humans, the 'built
environment' (cities) and the natural world.
The ideology developed in the late 19th century
in response to the rapid growth of cities and
industry in Western Europe and the United
States. Environmentalism tends to fall into several
different categories: conservation, preservation,
anti-pollution and environmental justice. 'Green
parties' incorporating environmental as well
as broader social justice issues have cropped
up around the world since the 1970s. The first
countries to have environmentally based parties
were Australia and New Zealand, followed by the
United Kingdom. The German party, *Die Grünen*
(The Greens), has been successful at the national
level, winning seats in their parliament and
offices in the government. Efforts to regulate
environmental standards on a more global level
have met with mixed results. The Kyoto Protocol,
adopted in 1997, currently commits 187 nations
and the European Community to reducing
emissions of greenhouse gases. However, the
United States has refused to sign the agreement
(although widely blamed for about 25 per cent
of the world's emissions), and no caps have
been set yet for heavily polluting nations such
as India and China.

3-SECOND SOUNDBITE
A broad political movement
that aims to protect the
Earth and its ecosystems
from potentially harmful
human actions.

3-MINUTE MANIFESTO
Environmentalism has
come under fire from
several groups: scientists
who dispute the evidence
of environmental
degradation and the dire
predictions of gloom and
doom (and are often
supported by polluting
industries), corporations
that feel environmental
regulation hurts
businesses and capitalism,
and costs jobs, as well as
others who feel that the
Earth has a far greater
regenerative capacity than
environmentalists believe.

RELATED THEORIES
See also
LIBERALISM
page 70
GLOBALIZATION
page 122

3-SECOND BIOGRAPHIES
JOHN MUIR
1838–1914
Naturalist, writer; instrumental
in establishing Yosemite
National Park

RACHEL CARSON
1907–1964
Author of *Silent Spring*;
described the dangers of
pesticides to the environment

AL GORE JR.
1948–
Politician; key in promoting
An Inconvenient Truth, the
documentary that spread
awareness of global warming

30-SECOND TEXT
Elizabeth D. Blum

*'When we try to pick
out anything by itself,
we find it hitched to
everything else in
the Universe.'*

JOHN MUIR

CONSTRUCTIVISM
the 30-second politics

Constructivism is a theory of international relations that argues that the international system is constructed by the interaction of states. Unlike realism, which focuses on individual state power and the lack of a world government, or liberalistic theories that focus on values and communication, constructivism examines the way in which the self-perceptions of states and their own understanding of the international environment shapes (or constructs) that environment. Specifically, constructivism states that rather than anarchy being an objective state of being in the international system it is the interaction of states and their perceived identities and interests that shape the international arena at a given moment in time (hence the notion that anarchy, and indeed the international system writ large, is 'what states make of it' – Alexander Wendt). Further, these interests and identities are socially constructed, that is they are the result of the interactions of states. In other words, the international system is not formed out of concrete, objective realities that then shape the options that states have within that system, but rather states themselves form the international system by their own practices. This implies that as the perceptions of states change over time so, too, will the international system change.

3-SECOND SOUNDBITE
International relations are not objective, but rather socially constructed.

3-MINUTE MANIFESTO
Constructivism is a relatively recent entry (its origins can be traced to the late 1980s/early 1990s) on the theoretical stage, coming into its own in the 1990s and 2000s. It has supplanted Marxist theories as the third major international relations theory (alongside realism and liberalism).

RELATED THEORIES
See also
NEOLIBERALISM
page 128
REALISM
page 138
IMPERIALISM
page 142
NEOCONSERVATISM
page 144

3-SECOND BIOGRAPHIES
NICHOLAS ONUF
1942–
Theorist credited with coining the term 'constructivism'

ALEXANDER WENDT
1958–
Theorist most associated with the constructivist school

30-SECOND TEXT
Steven L. Taylor

'The fundamental structures of international politics are social rather than strictly material.'
ALEXANDER WENDT

APPENDICES

NOTES ON CONTRIBUTORS

CONSULTANT EDITOR
Steven L. Taylor is a Professor of Political Science at Troy University, Alabama. He is the author of *Voting Amid Violence: Electoral Democracy in Colombia* and is currently working on a project comparing the United States to 29 other democracies. He has also contributed a number of the entries to this present volume.

WRITERS
Michael Bailey is an Associate Professor of Political Science at Berry College, Georgia. He has published book chapters and journal articles on the presidency, issues of church and state and democratic theory. He is married and has three daughters.

Elizabeth Blum is an Associate Professor of History at Troy University, Alabama. She completed her first book, *Love Canal Revisited: Race, Class, and Gender in Environmental Activism* in 2008. She is currently working on another project examining the variety of environmental messages in children's popular culture since the First World War.

G. Doug Davis is an Assistant Professor of Political Science at Troy University, Alabama. His interests include the international political economy, international relations, political methodology, ontology and Catholic theology.

Christopher N. Lawrence is an Assistant Professor of Political Science at Texas A&M International University at Laredo. He studies public opinion, voting behaviour and legislative politics in the United States and other advanced industrialized democracies, as well as the application of advanced statistical methods to political questions.

Feng Sung is an Assistant Professor in the Department of Political Science, Troy University, Alabama.

Gregory Weeks is an Associate Professor of Political Science and Director of Latin American Studies at the University of North Carolina at Charlotte. He is the author of numerous books and articles on Latin American politics, US-Latin American relations and immigration. He blogs on Latin American politics at http://weeksnotice.blogspot.com

RESOURCES

BOOKS

Anarchy, State and Utopia
Robert Nozick (Basic Books, 2006)

Antonio Gramsci
Steven J. Jones (Routledge, 2006)

Death of Nature: Women, Ecology and the Scientific Revolution Carolyn Merchant (HarperOne, 1990)

Dialectic of Enlightenment Max Horkheimer and Theodor W. Adorno (Verso Classics, 1997)

England's Treasure by Foreign Trade, 1664 Thomas Mun (BiblioBazaar, 2008)

The Enigma of Capital and the Crises of Capitalism David Harvey (Profile Books, 2010)

Evolution of Capitalism, The Philosophy of Misery: System of Economic Contradictions Pierre-Joseph Proudhon (Forgotten Books, 2008)

First Along the River: A Brief History of the US Environmental Movement Benjamin Kline (Rowman & Littlefield, 1997)

Forcing the Spring: The Transformation of the American Environmental Movement Robert Gottlieb (Island Press, 2005)

Free to Choose, Milton and Rose D. Friedman (Penguin Books, 1980)

The General Idea of Revolution in the Nineteenth Century Pierre-Joseph Proudhon (University Press of the Pacific, 2004)

The General Theory of Employment, Interest and Money John Maynard Keynes (BN Publishing, 2008)

History of Political Philosophy Leo Strauss and Joseph Cropsey (University of Chicago Press, 1987)

Imperialism: The Highest Stage of Capitalism Vladimir Lenin (Penguin Classics, 2010)

Introduction to Objectivist Epistemology Ayn Rand (Plume, 1990)

Making Sense of International Relations Theory Jennifer Sterling-Folker, ed. (Lynne Rienner, 2005)

Nature's Metropolis: Chicago and the Great West William Cronon (Norton, 1992)

On Democracy Robert A. Dahl (Yale University Press, 2000)

On Liberty J.S. Mill (Cambridge University Press, 1989)

The Philosophical Roots of Modern Ideology David E. Ingersoll, et al. (Longman, 2010)

Political Ideology: Why the American Common Man Believes What He Does Robert E. Lane (The Free Press, 1967)

BOOKS

Postmodernism, or, The Cultural Logic of Late Capitalism
Frederic Jameson (Verso Books, 1992)

The Poverty of Liberalism
Robert Paul Wolff (Beacon Press, 1968)

A Preface to Democratic Theory
Robert A. Dahl (University of Chicago Press, 2006)

The Prince Niccolo Machiavelli
(1513, Longman, 2003)

The Road to Serfdom F.A. Hayek
(Routledge, 2001)

Socialism and War G. Zinoviev and
Vladimir Lenin (1908, Kessinger, 2007)

The Spirit of Democracy: The Struggle to Build Free Societies Throughout the World
Larry Diamond (Times Books, 2008)

Taming the Prince Harvey C. Mansfield
(John Hopkins University Press, 1993)

A Theory of Justice John Rawls
(Harvard University Press, 2005)

The Un-Marxian Socialist: A Study of Proudhon Henri de Lubac
(Sheed & Ward, 1948)

The Virtue of Selfishness
Ayn Rand (Signet, 1992)

Wilderness and the American Mind
Roderick Nash (Yale University Press, 2001)

SELECTED eTEXTS
(cited by, or linked to, the entries):

The Communist Manifesto Karl Marx and Friedrich Engels
http://www.marxists.org/archive/marx/works/1848/communist-manifesto/

Critique of the Gotha Programme Karl Marx
http://www.marxists.org/archive/marx/works/1875/gotha/index.htm

Democracy in America Alexis de Tocqueville
http://www.gutenberg.org/ebooks/815

The Federalist Papers [also abbreviated to *The Federalist*] Alexander Hamilton, James Madison and John Jay
http://thomas.loc.gov/home/histdox/fedpapers.html

Nicomachean Ethics Aristotle
http://classics.mit.edu/Aristotle/nicomachaen.html

The Politics Aristotle
http://classics.mit.edu/Aristotle/politics.html

Reflections on the Revolution in France
Edmund Burke
http://www.bartleby.com/24/3/

The Second Treatise of Civil Government
John Locke
http://oregonstate.edu/instruct/phl302/texts/locke/locke2/2nd-contents.html

The Spirit of the Laws Baron de Montesquieu
http://etext.virginia.edu/toc/modeng/public/MonLaws.html

The Wealth of Nations Adam Smith
http://www.online-literature.com/adam_smith/wealth_nations/

USEFUL WEBSITES

Adam Carr's Electoral Archive
http://psephos.adam-carr.net/

The Avalon Project: Documents in Law,
History and Diplomacy
http://avalon.law.yale.edu/default.asp

Institute for Democracy and Electoral
Assistance (IDEA)
http://www.idea.int/index.cfm

The Internet Classics Library (MIT)
http://classics.mit.edu/index.html

Internet Modern History Sourcebook
http://www.fordham.edu/halsall/mod/
modsbook.html

Inter-Parliamentary Union
http://www.ipu.org/english/home.htm
(contains information on parliaments,
electoral systems and such).

Marxists Internet Archive Library
http://www.marxists.org/archive/index.
htm

Perseus Digital Library
http://www.perseus.tufts.edu/hopper/

Political Database of the Americas
http://pdba.georgetown.edu/

Richard Kimber's Political Science
Resources
http://www.politicsresources.net/

Stanford Encyclopedia of Philosophy
http://plato.stanford.edu/

Treehugger (environmental news and
blog site)
www.treehugger.com

INDEX

ACKNOWLEDGMENTS

PICTURE CREDITS
The publisher would like to thank the following individuals and organizations for their kind permission to reproduce the images in this book. Every effort has been made to acknowledge the pictures, however we apologize if there are any unintentional omissions.

Fotolia/Stephane Tougard: 110.
Getty Images/Ralph Morse/Time Life Pictures: 140.
Library of Congress, Prints and Photographs Division, Washington D.C.: 40, 43, 66, 88, 144bl.
Ludovisi Collection: 20.
Rex Features/CSU Archive/ Everett Collection: 130.